To my old mate :
Happy cooking!

Relish
SCOTLAND
THIRD HELPING

Original recipes from the region's finest chefs and restaurants. Featuring the Michelin starred chefs of Scotland.

First Published 2015
By Relish Publications
Shield Green Farm, Tritlington,
Northumberland, NE61 3DX.
Twitter: @Relish_Cookbook
Facebook: RelishRestaurantGuide

ISBN: 978-0-9575370-8-8

Publisher: Duncan L Peters
General Manager: Teresa Peters
Design: Vicki Brown
Relish Photography: Kevin Gibson (KGphotography)
and Nicky Rogerson (NRphotography)
Editorial Consultant: Paul Robertson
Proofing Coordinator: Valerie McLeod
Sales: Wendy Rutterford
Coordinator: Rebecca Laycock

Front cover photograph by: Paul Johnston
www.coppermango.com

Printed in Poland on behalf of Latitude Press

OUR HAND PICKED RESTAURANTS

As the proud owner of a Relish cookbook, you may subscribe for your own personal Relish Rewards card which entitles you to free membership for one year.

You can access the Relish members' area on our website and find out what exclusive offers are available to you from the fantastic restaurants featured in our series of books throughout the UK.

SUBSCRIBE FOR YOUR REWARD CARD ON OUR HOMEPAGE

Simply register your name, address and title of Relish book purchased to receive your **FREE Relish Reward Card**
www.relishpublications.co.uk

When you make a reservation, simply let the restaurant know that you are a member and take your card along with you.

WHAT ARE THE REWARDS?

The rewards will continue to be updated on the website so do check and keep in touch. These range from a free bottle of Champagne to free gifts when you dine. Relish will send you a quarterly newsletter with special discounts, rewards and free recipes. We are about quality not quantity!

All offers are subject to change. See the Relish website for details.

www.relishpublications.co.uk

004 CONTENTS

006 CONTENTS

Isle of Ewe Smoked Haddock Ravioli, Saffron Sauce, Leek Purée - **Page 312**

009 STARTERS

Zuppa Di Pesce (Italian Fish Stew) - **Page 248**

011 MAINS

Rhubarb With Flowers - **Page 044**

013 DESSERTS

014
THE ADAMSON RESTAURANT & BAR

127 South Street, St Andrews, Fife, KY16 9UH

01334 479 191
www.theadamson.com Twitter: @TheAdamson127 Facebook: The Adamson

Since opening in April 2012, The Adamson has built an excellent reputation for being the place to be for foodies and cocktail lovers in the centre of St Andrews. The former Post Office building is now a chic, contemporary, and vibrant restaurant that appeals to locals, visitors, golfers and students.

Managing director, Julie Lewis, is dedicated to hospitality, saying, "Our passion is to create a memorable dining experience for our guests, delivering excellence in quality of food and standard of service. Our chefs' creativity, combined with locally sourced produce and seasonal ingredients, is at the heart of all that we do."

Julie adds: "We receive fantastic feedback from guests, reviewers, critics and bloggers. To be included in the last three consecutive Michelin guides, as well as to hold 2 AA Rosettes, is testament to the dedication of our entire team." In 2014, The Adamson was also awarded 'Restaurant of the Year Scotland' by Food Awards Scotland and was 'highly commended' in the SLTN Awards.

And in 2015, the Year of Food and Drink in Scotland, The Adamson has expanded into a new cocktail and wine bar, offering unique cocktail creations and a selection of bar plates. It is a winning combination.

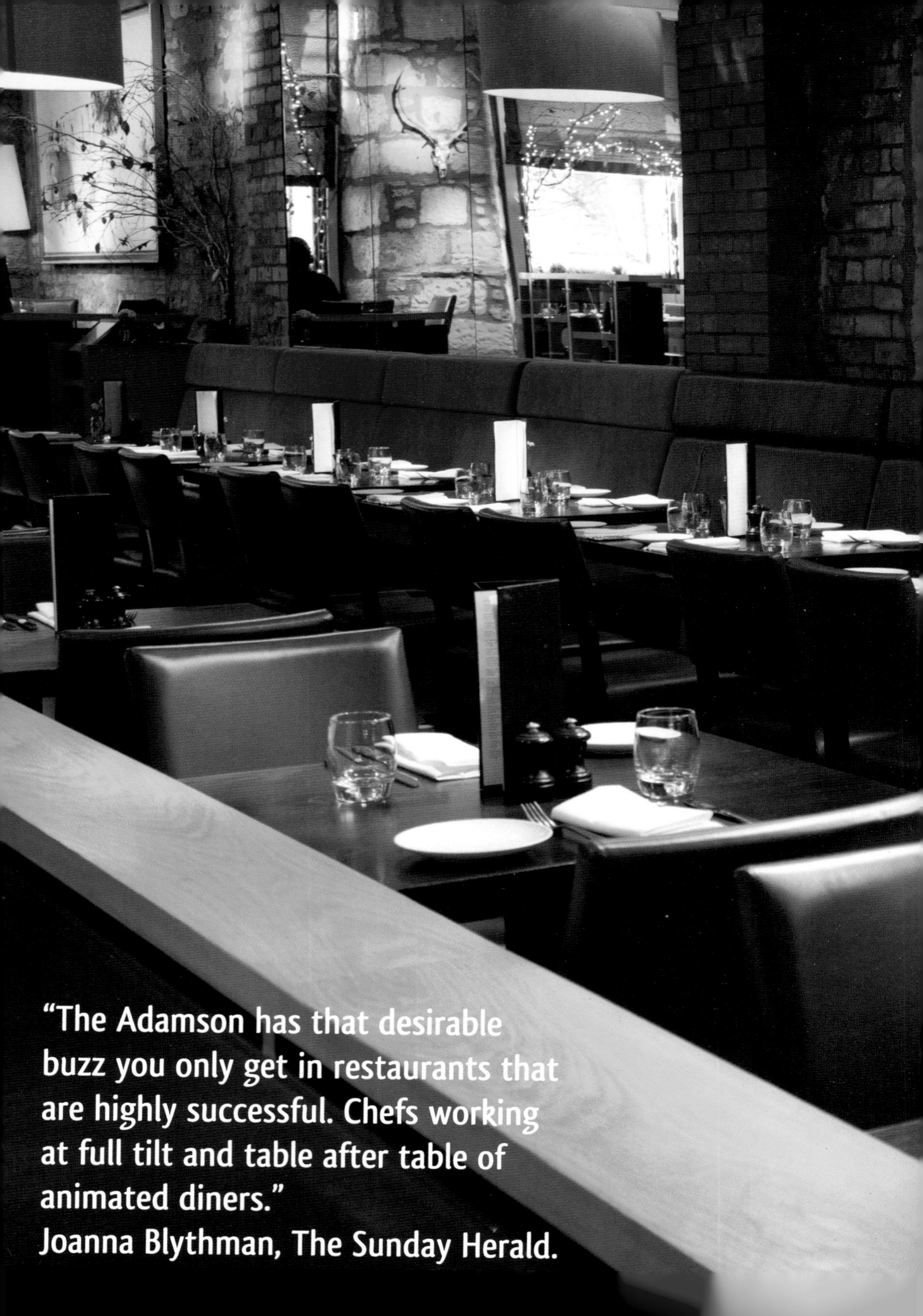
"The Adamson has that desirable buzz you only get in restaurants that are highly successful. Chefs working at full tilt and table after table of animated diners."
Joanna Blythman, The Sunday Herald.

QUAIL, SWEETCORN, SOY & MUSHROOM BROTH

SERVES 4

Consolation Antic, Rivesaltes Ambré 1985 (France)

Ingredients

Quail

2 whole quail (legs removed, seasoned)
400g duck fat
1 sprig thyme, sea salt
1 egg yolk, 50g plain flour, 50g fine breadcrumbs (to *panné*)

Soy And Mushroom Broth

50ml grape seed oil
2 large carrots (peeled, thinly sliced)
2 sticks celery (thinly sliced)
50g shallots (peeled, thinly sliced)
200g button mushrooms (thinly sliced)
200g flat cap mushrooms (thinly sliced)
2 sprigs thyme, 1 bay leaf, 12 peppercorns
1 litre chicken stock, 100ml light soy sauce

Onions

4 baby onions (peeled)
200ml pale ale, 2 sprigs thyme
1 clove garlic (lightly crushed)
salt (pinch of)

Corn On The Cob

1 corn on the cob (cooked)
50g butter
1 sprig thyme
1 clove garlic (lightly crushed)
10ml grape seed oil
sea salt (to taste)

Sweetcorn Purée

200g fresh sweetcorn kernels
200ml chicken stock, 100ml double cream
10ml lemon juice, sea salt (pinch of)

Garnish

4 quail eggs (cooked soft for 2 minutes, 22 seconds, then peeled and seasoned)
2 large chestnut mushrooms (thinly sliced)
25g oyster mushrooms
50g peas, 12 spears asparagus (*blanched*)

Method

For The Quail Legs

Place the legs, duck fat and thyme in a small pan, cover with tin foil and cook in an oven at 90°C (fan) for 2 hours, or until tender. Remove the legs from the fat. Remove the thigh bone and roll the leg into a sausage shape, using cling film. Cool in the fridge until firm, about 1 hour. Discard the cling film, roll the legs in the flour, followed by the egg and finally the breadcrumbs. Deep fry at 180°C for 2 minutes or until hot and golden.

For The Soy And Mushroom Broth

Add the oil, carrots, celery and shallots to a large pan over a high heat and cook for 5 minutes until golden brown. Stir in the button and flat cap mushrooms, herbs, peppercorns and a pinch of salt. Reduce the heat to medium and cook, covered, for 5 minutes. Add the stock and soy sauce, then cook for 10 minutes on a low heat. Pass through a muslin cloth and add more soy if needed. Keep hot.

For The Onions

Cook all the ingredients in a pan over a low heat for 10 minutes, or until just tender. Cool in the liquid. To serve, cut in half through the root and cook in a frying pan until dark brown.

For The Corn On The Cob

Add a little oil to an already hot frying pan and fry the cob on all sides until golden brown. Add the butter, thyme, a pinch of salt and the garlic and cook for 2 minutes on a low heat. Cut the kernels off the cob and keep warm.

For The Sweetcorn Purée

Gently cook the sweetcorn with the stock and salt until tender. Add the cream and reduce by half. Blitz until smooth and pass through a fine sieve. Finish the purée with lemon juice. Keep warm.

For The Quail Crowns

Preheat the oven to 160°C (fan).

Add a little oil to a hot frying pan and seal the quail on both skin sides until golden. Place the quail in breast-side up and cook in the oven for 6-8 minutes, or until the core temperature is 60°C. Leave to rest for 4 minutes. Remove the breasts from the crown, season and keep warm.

To Serve

Arrange the quail breast, leg and eggs in the centre of the plate. Place the corn in the middle, then add a couple of teaspoons of sweetcorn purée on the quail breast. Finish with the vegetables and finally, pour the broth over the top.

Chef's Tip

Samphire can be used in season instead of asparagus. The natural salt works really well with the dish.

(see glossary)

PLAICE, CURRIED CAULIFLOWER, NUTS & BROWN SHRIMP

SERVES 4

Calmel & Joseph Picpoul de Pinet, 2013 (France)

Ingredients

Plaice

4 x 120g thick plaice fillets (skinned, seasoned on one side)
25ml grape seed oil
50g butter
sea salt
½ lemon (juice of)

Cauliflower Purée

1 small cauliflower
25g unsalted butter
1 tbsp curry powder
salt (pinch of)
100ml chicken or vegetable stock
200ml double cream
½ lemon (juice of)

Curried Nuts, Cauliflower And Brown Shrimp Butter

100g unsalted butter
1 lemon (juice of)
1 tbsp curry powder
salt (pinch of)
25g macadamia nuts
50g blanched hazelnuts
50g whole blanched almonds
1 small cauliflower
25ml grape seed oil
100g brown shrimps (peeled)
1 tsp chives (finely sliced)
50g golden raisins (soaked in apple juice overnight)

Baby Gem Lettuce

2 heads baby gem lettuce (cut in half, washed)
300ml chicken or vegetable stock
25g butter
sea salt (pinch of)
black pepper (pinch of)

Method

For The Cauliflower Purée

Thinly slice the cauliflower head. Add the butter to a large saucepan over a medium heat and, once foaming, add the cauliflower, salt and curry powder. Cover with a lid, and cook on a low heat for 10 minutes, stirring every couple of minutes making sure it doesn't catch. Add the stock and double cream, reduce by half. Blitz the cauliflower until smooth, check the seasoning and add the lemon juice. Pass through a fine sieve. Keep hot.

For The Curried Nuts, Cauliflower And Brown Shrimp Butter

Start by making a curried butter. Melt the butter in a large frying pan over a low heat. Once melted, turn up the heat to high and cook until light brown. Add a pinch of salt, the lemon juice and curry powder, cook for 30 seconds. Pass through a muslin cloth.

Preheat the oven to 160°C (fan).

Roast the nuts in the oven for 6-8 minutes until lightly toasted. Leave to cool and crush before adding to the butter mixture.

Cut little florets from the cauliflower and roast them in the grape seed oil for 4-6 minutes until golden brown. Season and drain the oil off, then add to the curried butter with the brown shrimps, chives and golden raisins.

For The Baby Gem Lettuce

Bring the stock to the boil with a pinch of salt, pepper and the butter. Once boiling, add the baby gem lettuce, cover with a lid, and remove from the heat. Cook for 4 minutes until just tender. Remove the baby gems from the liquid and cut off the root. Season with salt and pepper. Keep warm.

For The Plaice

Heat a large non-stick frying pan over a high heat and once hot, add the oil. Gently put the plaice in, seasoned, side-down and cook for 2-3 minutes on a medium heat until golden brown. Turn the fish over, add the butter and cook for a further 2-3 minutes, depending on the thickness of the fillets, basting all the time. Finish with the lemon juice, remove from the pan and place on kitchen cloth.

To Serve

Swipe 3 spoonfuls of the purée on each plate. Arrange the lettuce in the centre of the plate with the plaice on top. Warm the curried butter up and split between the 4 plates, spooning over the fish.

SALTED CARAMEL BRULEE, BITTER CHOCOLATE, APPLE & HAZELNUTS

SERVES 4

Barrel Aged Old Fashioned Cocktail (bourbon, bitters, simple syrup and 1 week oak barrel aged)

Ingredients

Salted Caramel Brûlée

100g golden caster sugar
500ml double cream, 100g egg yolk (about 5 eggs)
1 whole egg, 2g sea salt
4 tsp golden caster sugar (to dust)

Chocolate Cream

100ml full-fat milk, 100ml double cream
40g egg yolk (about 2 eggs)
100g dark chocolate 70% (in chunks)

Aerated Chocolate

225g dark chocolate 53%, 45ml grape seed oil

Apple Sorbet (Prepare ahead)

250ml apple juice
½ lemon (juice of), 95ml stock syrup
Combine the ingredients, churn and freeze

Apple Purée

1 large Bramley apple (peeled, cored, roughly chopped)
50g unsalted butter
50g caster sugar, 50ml apple juice

Chocolate Crumble

15g cocoa powder, 50g plain flour
1g sea salt, 40g caster sugar
50g unsalted butter

Apple Cubes

1 Granny Smith apples (cut into 20 x 1cm cubes, cored and skin removed)
50g caster sugar, 20ml apple juice

Garnish

1 Granny Smith apple (cut into 20 thin sticks)
20g hazelnuts (lightly roasted, crushed)
2g celery cress (if desired)

4 x 6cmx5cm metal rings (lined tightly underneath with a double layer of cling film)
espuma/cream charger with 2 gas charges

Method

For The Salted Caramel Brûlée

Add 70g of sugar to a large pan over a high heat until it turns to a dark caramel colour - do not stir. Add the cream and slowly bring to a simmer. When simmering, whisk to ensure all the sugar has dissolved.

Combine the egg, yolks and remaining 30g of sugar in a large bowl and whisk. Pour the simmering cream over the egg mix, add the salt, then pass through a fine sieve. Leave to cool to room temperature.

Preheat the oven to 90°C (fan).

Place the moulds, cling film side down, onto a wet cloth lining an oven tray. Fill the moulds with the mix two thirds of the way up. Bake for 40 minutes, or until set. Cool in the fridge for 2 hours.

For The Chocolate Cream

Whisk together the milk, yolks and cream and cook over a low heat until it reaches 80°C. Pass through a fine sieve over the chocolate and let it stand for 5 minutes, then whisk until smooth. Pour into a piping bag and set in the fridge for 1 hour. Remove 10 minutes before serving.

For The Aerated Chocolate

Line a small, metal tray with greaseproof paper. Freeze for 1 hour. Melt the ingredients together in a *bain-marie* to 30°C. Pour into the charger and gas with 2 charges. Spray onto the tray and return to the freezer for 1 hour. Remove and break into 1cm squares. Keep in the fridge.

For The Apple Purée

Cook all the ingredients gently in a pan for 10 minutes until thick, stirring to make sure it does not catch. Blitz and check the flavour, adding more sugar if needed. Pass through a fine sieve, store in a squeezy bottle and place in the fridge for 20 minutes.

To Make The Chocolate Crumble

Rub all the ingredients together to a fine crumb. Bake on a metal tray for 25 minutes at 140°C (fan). Leave to cool, then break up using a fork.

For The Apple Cubes

Caramelise the sugar in a small frying pan. Once dark brown, add the apple and apple juice and cook for 1-2 minutes or until a syrup is formed. Leave to cool.

To Serve

Remove the brûlée from the moulds and plate them. Dust with 1 teaspoon of sugar and caramelise with a blow torch. Arrange the apple cubes, purée, chocolate cream and aerated chocolate around, then scatter with a tablespoon of chocolate crumble. Finish with a scoop of sorbet, hazelnuts, apple and celery cress.

(see glossary)

THE

MICHELIN STAR SPOTLIGHT...

JEFF BLAND

EXECUTIVE CHEF, NUMBER ONE AT THE BALMORAL

As executive chef at The Balmoral, I have spent the past 17 years ensuring that Number One provides our guests and visitors with exceptional dishes partnered with a memorable dining experience. Together with head chef Brian Grigor, I am passionate about Scotland's natural larder and spend much of my time sourcing the very finest of suppliers to showcase the incredible quality of produce from our shores. It is this produce which remains at the heart of the menu at Number One, with international ingredients such as Périgord truffle and Valrhona chocolate introduced to enhance the stand-out Scottish flavours.

Head chef Brian Grigor oversees the kitchen at Number One and restaurant director Gary Quinn oversees the front of house operations, complementing the dining experience with the very finest of 5 star service. Together we are incredibly proud to have retained a Michelin star for 13 consecutive years.

Surroundings play an integral part in the overall guest dining experience and I am delighted that Number One revealed an elegant new look in 2015 following a full refurbishment. The restaurant now features a fresh, contemporary style while retaining the warm and inviting atmosphere which guests have loved since the restaurant opened in 1997.

We are proud to be part of The Balmoral and Rocco Forte Hotels who continue to support our shared mission to deliver world-class Scottish hospitality to every guest.

Number One, The Balmoral, 1 Princes Street, Edinburgh, EH2 2EQ.
0131 557 6727 www.restaurantnumberone.com

026
THE AIRDS HOTEL & RESTAURANT

Port Appin, Appin, Argyll, PA38 4DF

01631 730 236
www.airds-hotel.com Twitter: airdshotel

The Airds has been privately owned and run for many years and is a member of Relais Chateaux and Pride of Britain. Located on the shores of Loch Linnhe with the backdrop of the Morvern mountains, you could not want for a more stunning and peaceful hideaway, with a welcoming ambience from the moment you arrive. With 11 individually decorated bedrooms and suites, many of them with spectacular loch and mountain views, and a two bedroom self catering cottage set within the grounds, there is a choice for everyone.

Enjoy full afternoon tea in one of the stylish lounges where a roaring fire in the winter will make you want to snuggle up with a good book or relax with an aperitif or indeed a night cap in the cosy bar, where there is an impressive display of Scottish whiskies just waiting to be tried. The garden stretches down to the loch where you can enjoy a simple stroll along the shoreline. For those feeling a little more energetic, a game of croquet or putting is on hand before sampling the delights of our canapés prior to dinner.

The restaurant has 3 AA Rosettes and a 'Gold Award' with Eat Scotland, making it one of the finest in the country. It uses fresh, seasonal ingredients and local produce - only the finest quality will do. The head chef leads an all Scottish kitchen brigade and also loves to develop apprentices - the next generation of chefs.

Breathtaking landscapes, incredible views down towards the loch, this remote and peaceful setting epitomises the west coast of Scotland. Surrounded by one of the best natural larders in the world, the best local produce is sourced wherever possible and the restaurant has been featured consistently in the Good Food Guide for 39 years.

PAN SEARED SCALLOPS WITH MANDARIN GEL, BEETROOT, SCALLOP TARTARE, FRESH TRUFFLE

SERVES 4

Côtes du Rhône Blanc, Les Becs Fins Tardieu-Laurent, 2012 (France)

Ingredients

Scallops

8 king scallops
rapeseed oil (to pan fry)
salt (to season)
1 lemon (juice of)
20g butter
brussel sprout leaves (handful of)

Scallop Tartar

½g fresh truffle
1 king scallop (diced into small pieces)
½ banana shallot (finely diced)
1 orange (zest of)
1 lemon (zest of)
1 lime (zest of)
truffle salt (to season)
1g powdered beetroot
salt and black pepper (to season)

Mandarin Gel

500g mandarin purée
10ml red wine vinegar
4g agar agar

To Serve

4 slices Iberico ham
1 small red beetroot
1 small yellow beetroot

Method

For The Scallop Tartar

Dice the truffle and combine with the scallop. Add the shallot, zest and truffle salt together with the beetroot powder. Season.

For The Mandarin Gel

Bring the purée to the boil. Stir in the vinegar and agar agar. Boil for 3 minutes, then remove from the heat and allow to set. Once set, blitz in the blender to a smooth gel.

For The Beetroot

Peel the beetroot, slice thinly with a knife or *mandolin*, then using a small round cutter, cut out discs.

For The Scallops

Preheat a non-stick pan. Season the scallops and pan fry on each side until golden. Add the butter, lemon juice and sprout leaves. Heat for 10 seconds then remove.

To Serve

Plate the cooked scallops. Add the scallop tartar and the remaining elements.

Chef's Tip

Always try to use hand dived scallops and as fresh as possible.

(see glossary)

SEARED VENISON, CHESTNUT GNOCCHI, PARSNIP & VANILLA PUREE, BLACKBERRY JUS, BABY VEGETABLES

SERVES 4

 *Pinot Noir, Eradus, Marlborough, 2011 (New Zealand)*

Ingredients

Venison

500g venison loin
2 sprigs rosemary

Chestnut Gnocchi

500g red rooster potatoes
100g chestnuts (peeled, *blanched*)
75g Parmesan
75g pasta flour
2 egg yolks
1 egg
salt and pepper (to season)

Parsnip And Vanilla Purée

1 parsnip (diced)
100ml milk
100ml double cream
20g butter
1 vanilla pod (seeds of)
salt (to season)

Blackberry Jus

15g blackberry purée
100ml veal stock

Baby Vegetables

12 baby carrots
1 red beetroot
1 yellow beetroot
3 large parsnips (trimmed to same size as carrots)

Chef's Tip

When searing the venison, do not have the pan too hot.

Method

For The Chestnut Gnocchi

Preheat the oven to 180°C (fan).

Roast the potatoes in the oven until soft in the centre. Roast the chestnuts for 10 minutes, leave to cool, then chop finely. Scoop out the potato and put into a bowl with the Parmesan and flour. Mix well, add the egg and yolks and mix together until it is fully *emulsified*. Add the chopped chestnuts.

For The Parsnip And Vanilla Purée

Place the parsnip in a pan with the milk, cream, butter, vanilla seeds and salt, and bring to the boil. Cook until the parsnip cubes are tender, and pass the mixture through a sieve.

For The Blackberry Jus

Bring the stock and purée to the boil. Remove from the heat and infuse for 10 minutes.

To Cook The Venison

Preheat the oven to 180°C (fan).

Brown the venison in a pan on both sides for no more than a couple of minutes. Transfer to the oven with the rosemary until it is cooked to your preference. For medium/rare, cook for 5-6 minutes. Slice the venison, allowing 3 pieces per portion.

To Serve

Place the venison on the plate, as pictured, with the purée, gnocchi and baby vegetables. Drizzle with the blackberry jus.

(see glossary)

CARROT CHEESECAKE WITH CARROT SORBET, CHOCOLATE SPONGE, CARROT RAVIOLI & CARAMEL TUILE

SERVES 8

Jurançon Domaine Cauhapé 2011 (France)

Ingredients

Carrot Sheet

150ml organic carrot juice
½ orange (juice of)
30g sugar
2g agar agar

Chocolate Sponge

2 medium eggs, 2 egg yolks
128g sugar
20g cocoa
110g plain flour
37g butter (melted)

Carrot Gel

200ml organic carrot juice
½ orange (juice of)
30g sugar
2g agar agar

Carrot Sorbet

125ml water
200g carrots (peeled, finely diced)
30g glucose
1 orange (juice of), 45g sugar

Carrot Cheesecake

60g egg yolk (about 3 eggs)
120g sugar
60ml organic carrot juice
200g mascarpone
100ml double cream
2½ leaves gelatine (soaked in cold water)

Caramel Tuile

200g isomalt (you can use sugar, but it won't give the same result)
50ml water

20cm cake tin (lined)

Method

For The Carrot Sheet

Blend the ingredients together and bring to the boil. Pour onto a flat tray to the thickness of about 2mm. Chill in the fridge.

For The Chocolate Sponge

Preheat the oven to 190°C (fan).

Whip the eggs and sugar over a pot of simmering water until frothy. Continue to whip in a stand mixer until tripled in volume. Fold in the flour and cocoa powder, adding the butter last. Pour into the cake tin and bake for 20-25 minutes.

For The Carrot Cheesecake (Allow time to set)

Beat the yolks in a mixer on medium speed. Boil the sugar and carrot juice to 121°C, then pour in a thin, steady stream over the yolks and whip on high speed until maximum volume is achieved. Squeeze excess water from the gelatine, add to the yolk mix and whip until cool. Fold in the softened mascarpone and gently fold in the cream. Set in the fridge for 2 hours. Once set, return to a blender and blend until smooth. Transfer to a piping bag. Spread a double layer of cling film on a kitchen surface, pipe lines of cheesecake and roll tightly in the cling film. Tie each end and return to the fridge for 1 hour.

For The Carrot Gel

Blend the juices, sugar and agar agar together and bring to the boil. Remove any scum, then set on a flat tray in the fridge. Once set, blend until smooth.

For The Carrot Sorbet

Combine all the ingredients in a pan and gently poach until the carrot is very soft. Blend until smooth, then pass through a fine sieve. Cool, then churn in an ice cream machine.

For The Caramel Tuile

Boil the isomalt and water to 160°C, pour onto a silicone mat and leave until cool. Blend to a fine powder. Preheat the oven to 160°C (fan). Sprinkle in the desired shapes on a silicone mat and cook for about 2 minutes. Cool and reserve in an airtight container.

To Serve

Carefully wrap the carrot sheet around the cheesecake and serve as pictured.

Chef's Tip

You can make all elements of this dish in advance.

036
THE ATELIER

159-161 Morrison Street, Haymarket, Edinburgh, EH3 8AG

0131 629 1344
www.theatelierrestaurant.co.uk Twitter: @theatelierinfo

The Atelier is a wonderful little restaurant in the heart of Haymarket - Edinburgh's best place for fine food, fine wine, and a friendly atmosphere that's always buzzing, never crowded. It's relaxed at The Atelier. All our finery is in the kitchens. Casual enough for an impromptu lunch yet intimate enough for a special occasion. Business day or leisurely evening, it has to be The Atelier Restaurant.

The Atelier Restaurant provides modern European food with a Scottish accent. Travel broadens the mind. Maciek Zielinski, our gourmet, has galloped all over the continent to bring the best of contemporary cosmopolitan Europe back to Scotland, back to The Atelier Restaurant. He has flavoured his finest finds with a touch of Caledonian innovation and served up a menu to tempt, savour and delight.

Maciek learned his profession right here in Edinburgh. He was hard at work, nearer to ground level. If you've ever pulled on a chef's whites, you'll have heard of Maciek. In a business where you're only as good as your last creation, that's what counts really, reputation.

'"Consistency is important, in service and food. I want to see every guest, every diner, get the best, every time. It has to be the best standard, consistently," says Maciek.

From royalty to the richest, Maciek has run busy kitchens for them all, in places as diverse as Norway's famous Hall Toll. He counts Scandinavian Stephan Anderson and American Charlie Palmer among his mentors. You can just count on him to have learned from the best and matured into a bit of a celebrity himself.

Maciek says: "I could see the cruise ships out at sea. When I worked the small luxury ships, we'd have the most demanding clients. It sets a standard you never drop, it stays with you."

The whole Atelier team is proud to have been acknowledged in The List Drinking & Eating 2014/15 as 'Newcomer of the Year' after being open for only seven months. And the success and momentum hasn't stopped, now holding 2 AA Rosettes and delighted to make it to the 2015/16 edition of The Michelin Guide.

VENISON HAGGIS, NEEPS & TATTIES

SERVES 4

 *Corbieres, Château La Condamine, Languedoc (France)*

Ingredients

Venison

200g piece venison loin
50ml gin
1 sprig rosemary
2 cloves garlic (chopped)
oil (to fry)

Venison Haggis Bon Bons

180g venison haggis
50g panko breadcrumbs
25g dry gingerbread (blended to powder)
3 eggs (beaten)
25g flour
oil (to shallow fry)

Potatoes

100g purple potatoes
20g unsalted butter
50ml double cream
salt and pepper (to season)

Baby Turnip

1 bunch baby turnips (washed)
150ml water
25g unsalted butter
3g salt

Pickled Turnip

1 small turnip (thinly sliced)
25g caster sugar
25g white wine vinegar
50g water
1 star anise
1 sprig thyme, 1 small bay leaf
½ tsp turmeric

Garnish

gin jus, radish
salted turnip purée
brussel sprout leaves
pear fluid gel, pear crisps
micro rocket

Method

For The Venison

Marinate the venison with the garlic, gin and rosemary, cover and place in the fridge for 2 hours. Heat a little oil in a pan and fry the venison all sides for 2 minutes. Finish it in a preheated oven (180°C fan) for 5 minutes. Rest on a cooling rack.

For The Venison Haggis Bon Bons

Divide the haggis into 20g balls. Mix the panko breadcrumbs and gingerbread together. Toss the balls in the flour, then beaten eggs and finish with the mixture of panko and gingerbread. Repeat, but this time only tossing with eggs, then breadcrumbs. Shallow fry in a pan until golden and crispy.

For The Potatoes

Boil the potatoes in salted water, with the skin still on, until soft in the middle. Peel when still warm, then mash. Heat the cream and butter in a pan and stir in the mashed potatoes. Season and mix to a smooth texture.

For The Baby Turnip

Cut the stems from the turnips, reserving 1½ cm of the tops (green part). Bring to the boil in the water, with the butter and salt. Cook for 4 minutes, then cool in iced water.

For The Pickled Turnip

Bring all the ingredients, apart from the turnip, to the boil and set aside.

Cut small rings from the turnip slices using pastry cutters. Add the turnip circles to the warm marinade. Cover and pickle for 2 hours.

To Serve

Carve the venison into slices and arrange on the plate with the other elements as per the picture. Garnish with as many of the garnishes as you wish.

MILK POACHED HALIBUT, CRISPY PANCETTA, SQUID INK PASTA, MOREL SAUCE, SEA HERB SALAD

SERVES 4

Oaked Chardonnay Reserva, De Martino, Limari, Valley (Chile)

Ingredients

Halibut

4 x 150g halibut fillets
1 litre water (iced)
50g salt
1 litre milk
4g lemon thyme sprigs
1 bay leaf
3 cloves garlic
6 black peppercorns

Morel Sauce

175ml good red wine
175ml good quality chicken stock
5g dried morel mushrooms
25g unsalted butter
salt and pepper (to taste)

Pancetta Powder

150g unsmoked pancetta

Squid Ink Pasta

300g universal flour (high gluten content)
½ tsp salt
10g squid ink
1 egg yolk
40ml double cream
225g mascarpone cheese

Sea Herb Salad

sea fennel
sea beetroot
sea rosemary
parsley, lemon oil (to dress)

Garnish

fish velouté

Method

For The Morel Sauce (Prepare ahead)

Soak the morel mushrooms overnight in water.

Bring the wine and stock to the boil and reduce by three quarters. Whisk in the butter and add the sliced mushrooms. Season to taste.

For The Halibut

Steep the halibut for 30 minutes in a brine made from the water and salt.

Bring all the other ingredients to the boil and simmer for 15 minutes to infuse the flavours.

Remove the halibut from the brine, wash and pat dry. Remove the infused milk from the heat, carefully add in the halibut and poach for 6-8 minutes, depending on the thickness of the fish.

For The Pancetta Powder

Cut the pancetta into lardons. Fry in a heavy bottomed pan until crispy, then drain off all the fat. Dry the pancetta with paper, then blitz in a food processor to a powder.

For The Squid Ink Pasta

Mix the wet ingredients together and add to the flour with the salt. Knead in the mascarpone cheese to form a dough. Place the dough in the fridge for 30 minutes. Once ready, roll the dough into 1½cm thick strips, then cut into 3cm pieces.
Boil the pasta in a pot of salted water until the pasta rises to the top, then simmer for a further 3 minutes.

For The Sea Herb Salad

Combine the ingredients and dress with the lemon oil.

To Serve

Serve as pictured, dusted with the pancetta crumb and dotted with the fish velouté.

RHUBARB WITH FLOWERS

SERVES 4

Late Harvest, Gewürztraminer, Montes, Colchagua (Chile)

Ingredients

Gorse Custard

250ml double cream, 50ml milk
3 egg yolks, 1 egg, 30g sugar
30g gorse flowers

Fennel Seed Financiers

200g butter
50g fennel seeds
250g icing sugar, 83g plain flour
83g ground almonds
20g good quality honey
167g egg whites (from 4-5 eggs)
1 vanilla pod (seeds of, reserve pod)

Elderflower Marshmallows

90ml elderflower cordial
35ml lemon juice
24g gelatine sheets (soaked in cold water)
2 egg whites, 500g sugar, 200ml water

Rhubarb Turkish Delight Fluid Gel

80g honey, 100g sugar
325g rhubarb (sliced)
1 lemon (zest of)
40ml lemon juice
300ml water
50ml rose water
8g agar agar

Rhubarb Tagliatelle

500ml water, 300g sugar
1 empty vanilla pod (reserved from financier mix)
280g rhubarb

Lavender Poached Rhubarb

325g rhubarb (cut into 2cm pieces)
165g sugar, 4g dried lavender flowers
300ml water

Garnish

hibiscus caviar, pink peppercorn meringues
rhubarb sorbet, edible flowers

financier mould tin

Method

For The Gorse Custard

Bring the cream, milk and gorse to a simmer and infuse for 20 minutes. Whisk the yolks, egg and sugar together. Add the warm cream mix to the egg mix. Return to the heat, whisking continuously, until the mixture reaches 85°C. Pour the custard through a fine sieve and refrigerate until required.

For The Fennel Seed Financiers

Heat the fennel seeds in the butter until it starts to foam, pass through a sieve and allow to cool. Combine the sugar, flour, almonds, honey, egg whites and vanilla seeds in a bowl. Mix to a batter consistency and gradually add 167g of the butter. Refrigerate for 4 hours. Pipe the batter into moulds and cook in a preheated oven at 185°C for 15 minutes.

For The Elderflower Marshmallows

Squeeze excess water from the gelatine and place in a pan with the cordial and lemon juice.

Boil the sugar and water to 121°C in a separate pan. Whisk the egg whites in an electric mixer and pour the sugar mix onto the egg whites while still whisking. Warm the cordial, juice and gelatine until the gelatine has melted, then add to the meringue mixture.

Once the mixture has cooled a little, transfer it to a shallow baking tray, greased with vegetable oil. Refrigerate until set for 2 hours. Cut into desired shapes.

For The Rhubarb Turkish Delight Fluid Gel

Place all of the ingredients in a pan and simmer until the rhubarb is cooked. Chill in the fridge for 2 hours, until set. Blend in a food processor to a smooth gel. Keep in the fridge.

For The Rhubarb Tagliatelle

Shave the rhubarb into long strips using a peeler. Bring the water, sugar and vanilla pod to the boil and pour on top of the shaved rhubarb. Put a lid on top of the container and allow to cool. Place in the fridge until required.

For The Lavender Poached Rhubarb

Place all the ingredients in a pan and heat until the rhubarb is cooked.

To Serve

Serve as pictured

MICHELIN STAR SPOTLIGHT...

GRAEME CHEEVERS & MARTIN WISHART

MARTIN WISHART AT LOCH LOMOND

I was invited in November 2008, by the directors of Cameron House Resort, to open my second restaurant at the world renowned Cameron House Hotel on the bonnie banks of Loch Lomond. Cameron House is a wonderful retreat, a world class hotel, a romantic and unforgettable escape with stunning loch views.

Along with head chef Graeme Cheevers and restaurant manager Mark Patonyi, I have been directing the team at Cameron House for over six years. Since then, we have seen its reputation grow and achieved Scottish Restaurant of the Year 2009, 3 AA Rosettes since 2010 and a Michelin star since 2012.

Our menu is designed to offer the customer a large variety of seasonal ingredients. Many of these ingredients are sourced locally, such as pike from Loch Lomond, langoustines and crab from the Isle of Skye and grouse, partridge and venison, when in season, from Ayrshire, as well as lamb and beef from the Borders.

The restaurant's front of house staff are professionally directed by Mark Patonyi, a long standing, senior manager from the Edinburgh restaurant and one of Scotland's most charming maître d's. Mark has now been working at Martin Wishart for over seven years, having started as a waiter in the Edinburgh restaurant back in 2008.

The wines form an extensive and varied list of exceptional and affordable vintages from all over the world and are stored in the beautiful cellar which can be viewed from the restaurant. The wine list is managed by our sommelier Peter Convery.

Martin Wishart at Loch Lomond is every bit as luxurious as its sister restaurant in Leith, both restaurants sharing a similar ethos and style throughout.

Cameron House, Loch Lomond, Dunbartonshire, G83 8QZ.
01389 722 504 www.martin-wishart.co.uk

048 BALLATHIE HOUSE HOTEL & ESTATE

Kinclaven, Stanley, Perthshire, PH1 4QN

01250 883 268
www.ballathiehousehotel.com Twitter: @ballathiehouse

The advice, when at Ballathie, is "drink in the scenery, then eat it". This could not be more appropriate since Ballathie is surrounded by an abundant larder; lush, green pastures graze pedigree cattle and sheep which are destined for the Ballathie kitchen, along with local game from the Estate and seasonal fresh vegetables grown on the Ballathie Farm. There is ample foraging ground, just a stone's throw from the kitchen, offering wild mushrooms and wild garlic.

The Restaurant at Ballathie House Hotel has possibly one of the most scenic outlooks, overlooking the famous River Tay. The dining experience is relaxed, diners still dine from Villeroy and Boch plates, but simple in their style, without any fashion statement, traditional slate, glass and vintage silver cutlery, all deliberately understated to allow the food to make its own statement.

Chef Scott Scorer takes great pride in personally selecting the best possible ingredients and often visits growers and producers to see the origin of the produce selected for his kitchen.

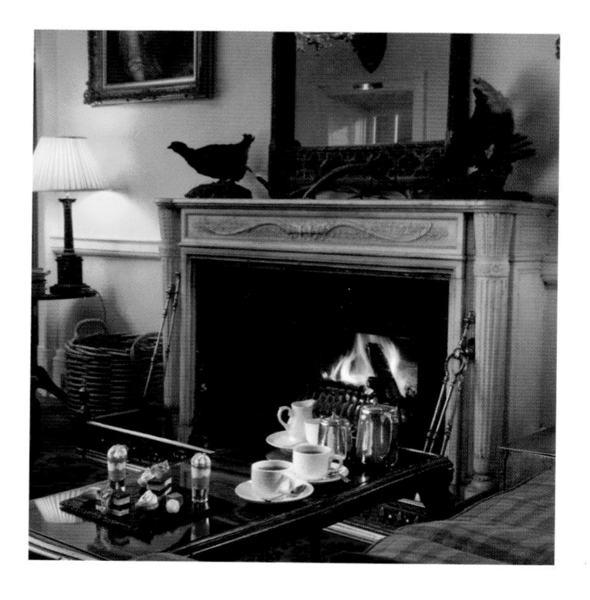

He encourages his brigade to spend a day in the life of the gamekeeper, the ghillie, the cattleman, the local market gardener, all of which helps the younger chef's understanding of the dedication that goes into the growing and harvesting of the produce destined for the kitchen. Thus their respect for ingredients inspires them to create fabulous dishes with care and appreciation.

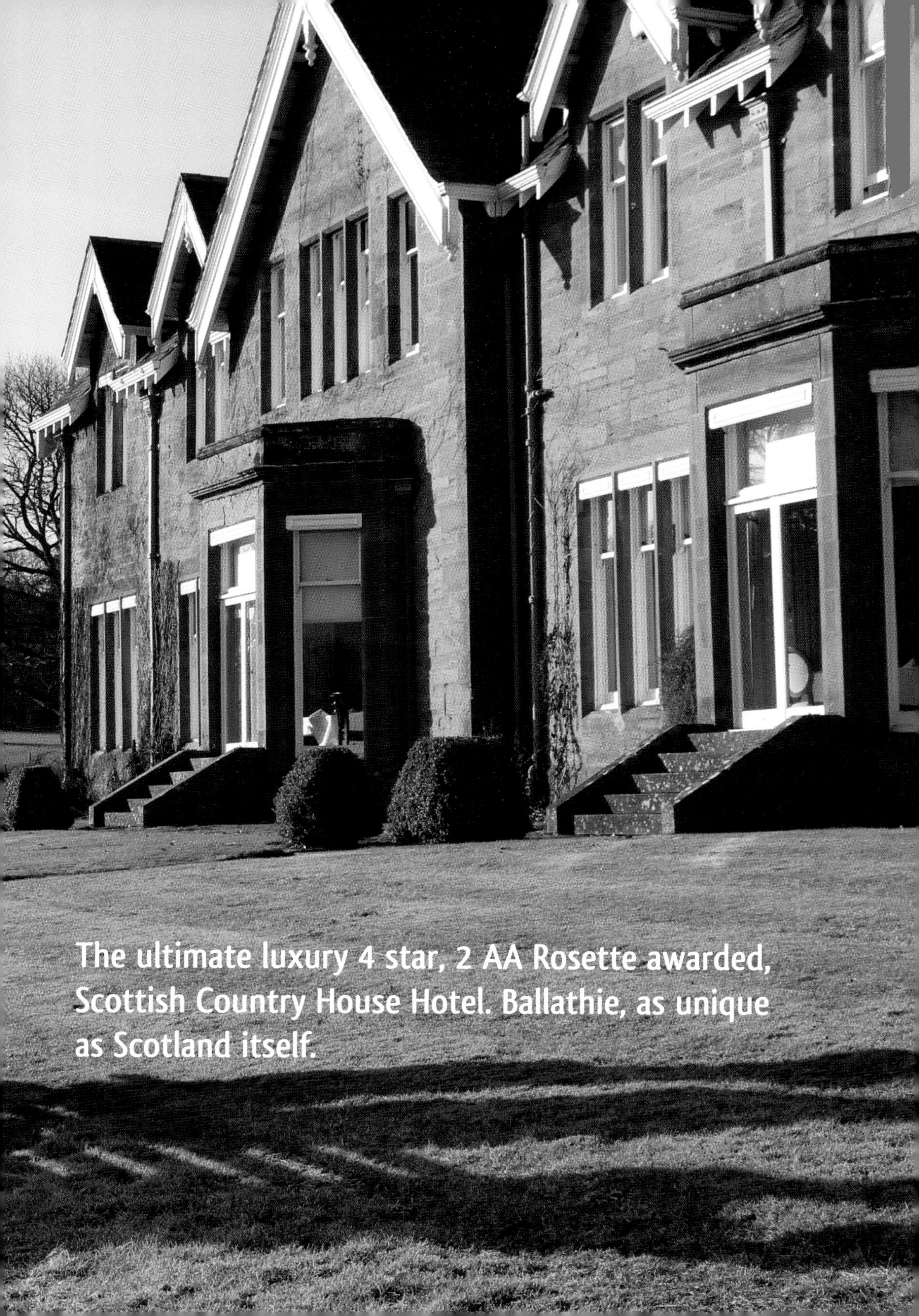
The ultimate luxury 4 star, 2 AA Rosette awarded, Scottish Country House Hotel. Ballathie, as unique as Scotland itself.

TERRINE OF SALMON & SOLE, WASABI MAYONNAISE, SMOKED SALMON, GRANARY CROUTE

SERVES 8

Chablis, Domaine Vincent Dampt (France)

Ingredients

Terrine Of Salmon And Sole

5 Witch sole fillets
500g fresh salmon
16 crevettes
court bouillon (to poach)
1 lemon (zest and juice of)
100g cream cheese
2g parsley (chopped)
30g clarified butter
salt and pepper

Wasabi Mayonnaise

100g mayonnaise
4g wasabi paste

Lemon Dressing

200ml rapeseed oil
10 lemons (juice of)
2g xanthan gum

Salmon And Nori Roulade

1 slice 'long sliced' smoked salmon
50g cream cheese
2 sheets nori

Granary Croûte

4 slices granary bread (crusts off)
10ml rapeseed oil
salt and pepper (to season)

Compressed Cucumber

1 cucumber (sliced into batons, seeds removed)
salt (pinch of)
sugar (pinch of)
1 tsp lemon juice

Garnish

Avruga caviar

terrine mould (lined with cling film)

Method

For The Terrine Of Salmon And Sole

Poach the salmon and sole in the *court bouillon*. In the last 3 minutes of cooking add the crevettes, cool and peel, then put to one side for assembly of the dish.

Once the salmon and sole are cooked, remove from the heat and cool. Flake the poached salmon and sole into a bowl, add the cream cheese, lemon zest, juice and parsley. Add the clarified butter and season with salt and pepper. Fold together and press into the prepared mould.

To Make The Wasabi Mayonnaise

Mix the ingredients until fully combined.

For The Lemon Dressing

Reduce the juice of the lemons to a syrup. Slowly pour in the rapeseed oil and add the xanthan gum. Mix well and set aside. This dressing will keep for 2 weeks.

To Make The Salmon And Nori Roulade

Place a layer of cling film on your workbench. Place the smoked salmon on top, spread the cream cheese on the salmon and finally place the sheet of nori on top of the cream cheese. Roll up tightly into a cylinder. Chill until ready to serve, then slice with a sharp knife.

To Make The Granary Croûte

Preheat the oven to 180°C (fan).

Roll the granary bread through a pasta machine until really thin. Cut each slice each into 4 rectangles, season, spread with rapeseed oil, then place in the oven. Cook until crisp, for approximately 5 minutes.

To Make The Compressed Cucumber

Combine the ingredients and put into a vac pack machine, then compress for 30 minutes. Sear quickly to add colour.

To Serve

Cut the terrine into rectangular slices. Assemble the rest of the elements on top of the terrine with dots of the dressings lengthways on each side and sandwich with the granary croûte.

(see glossary)

LOIN OF VENISON, BUTTERNUT SQUASH FONDANT, VENISON CHORIZO CASSEROLE

SERVES 4

Chateauneuf-du-Pape Grande Reserve, Château Beauchêne (France)

Ingredients

Loin Of Venison

600g loin of venison (cut into 4)
salt and pepper
butter (knob of)

Venison Chorizo Casserole

10ml olive oil
15g butter
1 onion (diced)
2 fresh garlic cloves (crushed)
175g venison chorizo (diced)
250g mushrooms (halved)
1¼kg haunch or shoulder of venison (diced)
¼ bottle red wine
200ml venison stock
1½ tbsp redcurrant jelly
salt and freshly ground black pepper (to taste)
25g plain flour
3 juniper berries (crushed)

Pommes Anna

1kg waxy potatoes (peeled, very thinly sliced)
225g butter (melted)
salt and pepper

Butternut Squash Fondant

1 butternut squash (peeled, diced into 1½cm cubes)
25g butter
200ml chicken stock

To Serve

1 punnet blackberries
1 head curly kale
tenderstem broccoli

4 ramekin dishes

Method

For The Loin Of Venison

Preheat the oven to 180°C (fan).

Pan sear the loin, then place in the oven for 8 minutes. Remove from the oven, sprinkle with salt and pepper and a knob of butter, baste for 30 seconds, then leave to rest for 5 minutes.

For The Venison Chorizo Casserole

Preheat the oven to 150°C (fan).

Heat the olive oil and butter in a large, lidded casserole dish on the hob. Add the onion and cook until softened, but not browned. Stir in the garlic, venison chorizo and mushrooms and cook for a further minute.

Toss the venison haunch or shoulder in flour, then brown, a handful at a time, in a frying pan. Add to the casserole. Add the red wine, stock, redcurrant jelly, salt and pepper and juniper berries. Bring to the boil and stir well. Cover and cook in the oven for 90 minutes. Set aside.

For The Pommes Anna

Preheat the oven to 200°C (fan).

Put the potato slices in a colander and rinse under cold water. Pat dry with a cloth.

Grease a sheet of greaseproof paper and arrange the potato slices on the paper in overlapping circles, brushing the butter over each layer, seasoning as you go. Cover with another sheet of greaseproof paper and bake in the oven for 30 minutes, or until the potatoes are cooked.

For The Butternut Squash Fondant

Preheat the oven to 180°C (fan).

Place the butternut squash in a non-stick pan with the butter, lightly colour all sides, and season. Add the stock and place in the oven for 20 minutes or until tender.

To Assemble

Divide the casserole into 4 ramekins (this will leave you plenty left over which you can enjoy the next day or freeze!), then top with the pommes Anna. Place in the oven at 180°C (fan) for a further 5 minutes, before serving.

Slice the venison loin into 3 collops and plate opposite the casserole. Arrange the other elements as pictured.

RHUBARB & CUSTARD SOUFFLE, RHUBARB RIPPLE ICE CREAM

SERVES 8

Château Septy Monbazillac (France)

Ingredients

Rhubarb Jam

400g rhubarb (cut to 3cm pieces)
100g caster sugar
1 orange (zest of)

Rhubarb Ripple Ice Cream

500ml milk
500ml double cream
2 vanilla pods (split lengthways)
12 egg yolks
200g caster sugar

Panard

200g rhubarb purée
40g caster sugar
1¼ tsp cornflour

Custard

500ml milk
500ml double cream
1 vanilla pod (seeds scraped)
10 egg yolks
150g caster sugar

Soufflé

180g panard (as above)
200g pasteurised egg whites
120g caster sugar
icing sugar (to dust)

Garnish

shortbread crumbs

8 ramekin moulds (buttered, ensuring the strokes are going up with the ramekin)

Method

For The Rhubarb Jam (Prepare ahead)

Preheat the oven to 130°C (fan).

Toss the rhubarb pieces in a bowl with the sugar and orange zest. Transfer to a baking dish, cover with foil and bake for 45 minutes until completely tender. Remove from the oven and allow to cool for 1 hour. Transfer the rhubarb to a heavy bottomed pan and cook to a rich jam.

For The Rhubarb Ripple Ice Cream (Prepare ahead)

Heat the milk, cream and vanilla in a saucepan and bring to the boil.

Whisk the egg yolks and sugar together until pale and fluffy.

Pour the boiling milk and cream over the egg yolk mixture to make a custard. Place back on the heat until it coats the back of a spoon. Pass through a fine sieve, chill, then churn in an ice cream machine. Once churned, fold 150g of the rhubarb jam through to create a ripple effect, then freeze.

For The Panard

Combine 160g of the rhubarb purée with the sugar in a pan, and bring to the boil.

Mix together the remaining purée with the cornflour. Add to the hot mixture, bring back to the boil, then chill.

For The Custard

Heat the milk, cream and vanilla in a saucepan and bring to the boil.

Whisk the egg yolks and sugar together in a bowl.

Gradually add the boiled cream to the egg yolk mixture, continually whisking until it coats the back of a spoon.

To Make The Soufflé

Preheat the oven to 170°C (fan).

Whisk together the egg whites and caster sugar until soft peaks, then fold the panard through the mixture.

Place the soufflé mixture into a piping bag and pipe into the moulds ensuring they come approximately ½cm above the rim. Level off with a palette knife, then run your thumb around the outside of the mixture to leave a groove. Bake for 7-8 minutes.

Chef's Tip

It's best to use pasteurised egg whites for the soufflé.

To Serve

Carefully remove the soufflé from the oven, dust with icing sugar, then place on the plate. Fill a small jug with the custard and finish with shortbread crumbs and a *quenelle* of rhubarb ripple ice cream on top.

(see glossary)

058

BISTRO MODERNE BY MARK GREENAWAY

15 North West Circus Place, Edinburgh, EH3 6SX

0131 225 4431
www.bistromoderne.co.uk Twitter: @bistromoderne Facebook: Bistro Moderne

Bistro Moderne by Mark Greenaway is an original concept in bistro dining from the award-winning chef, taking the classic concept and revitalising it with the imaginative dishes Mark is known for.

The term 'bistro moderne' originated in France. Those who trained under the top chefs at some of the best restaurants normally housed in grand hotels, eventually moved to the suburbs to establish their own businesses. They set up small restaurants and bistros. A 'bistro moderne' represented an establishment which served amazing food but in a more relaxed and informal way. Using the skills and ingredients honed during their time in restaurant kitchens, they then adapted these to suit their more laid-back bistros. Bistro Moderne by Mark Greenaway is situated just north of Edinburgh's New Town in the striking suburb of Stockbridge.

They offer a dining experience borrowed from these rural restaurants of France, serving light lunches, à la carte dinners, Sunday roasts and a five course grazing menu, all of which can be paired with wine, cocktails and whisky.

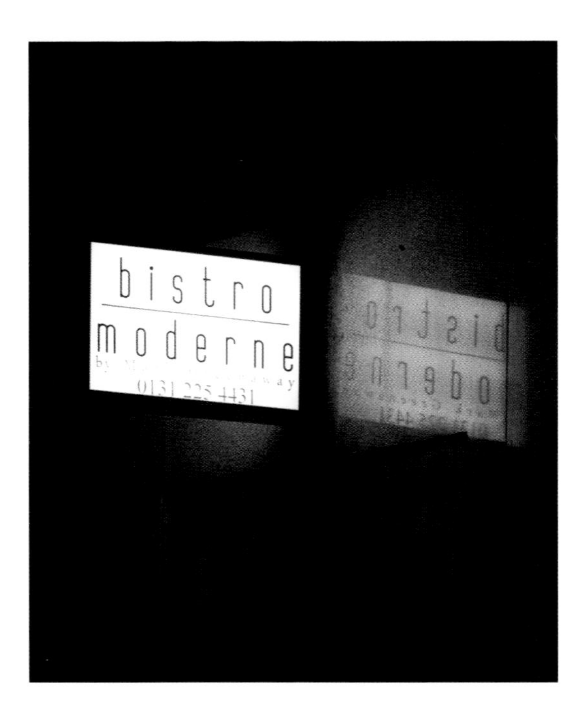

The ethos is to use seasonal ingredients from Scotland, giving them the playful, modern twist that only Mark Greenaway can do.

Bistro Moderne food images: Paul Johnston www.coppermango.com

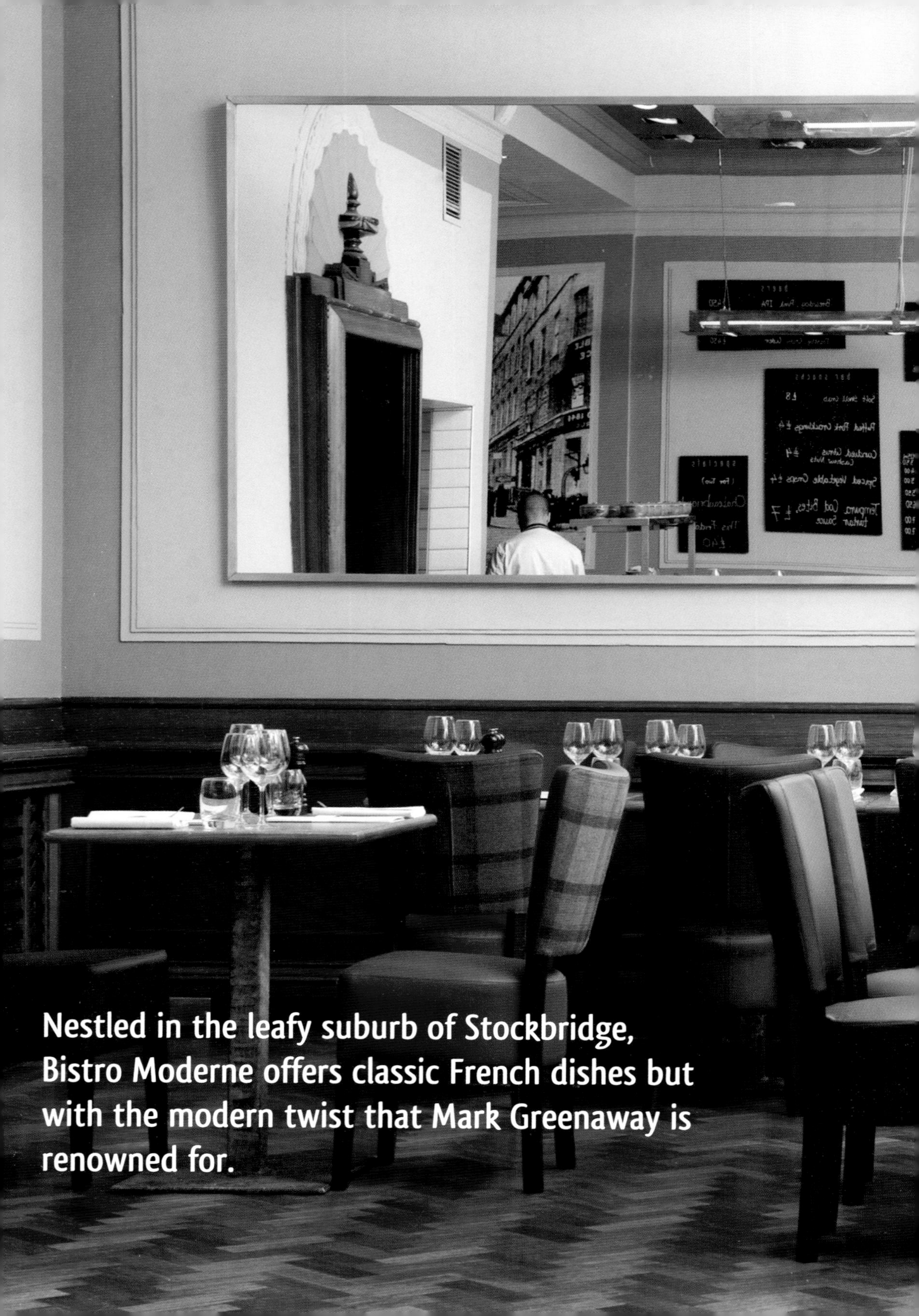

Nestled in the leafy suburb of Stockbridge, Bistro Moderne offers classic French dishes but with the modern twist that Mark Greenaway is renowned for.

HOT SMOKED SALMON, APPLE, WATERMELON, HAZELNUTS & SAFFRON MAYONNAISE

SERVES 4

Dry Sparkling Riesling, 2010, Skillogalee, Clare Valley (Australia)

Ingredients

Hot Smoked Salmon

400g salmon (pin-boned, skin off)
200g salt
400g caster sugar
1 lime (zest and juice of)
1 orange (zest and juice of)
5 star anise
2 tbsp dill (chopped)

Saffron Mayonnaise

1 whole egg
1 egg yolk
1 tsp Dijon mustard
2 tbsp sherry vinegar
saffron (large pinch of, soaked in 3 tbsp boiling water)
500ml rapeseed oil

Apple, Watermelon And Hazelnut Salad

1 apple (thinly sliced)
½ cucumber (thinly sliced)
½ watermelon (peeled, cubed)
hazelnuts (handful of, chopped)
micro herbs

For The Smoker

wood chips
1 cooling rack
1 old baking tray

Method

For The Salmon (Prepare ahead)

Blend all of the ingredients together, excluding the salmon. Smother the salmon with the rub, cover and store in the fridge for 12 hours.

Rinse the rub from the salmon.

Place the wood chips on the baking tray and top with the wire rack.

Arrange the salmon on the wire rack and cover in tin foil. Place the tray on the hob over a medium heat and smoke for 7-8 minutes, or until the salmon is medium rare.

For The Saffron Mayonnaise

In a bowl or the container of a food processor, combine the egg, egg yolk, mustard, vinegar, saffron and water.

Set the food processor on medium speed, or whisk by hand, and gradually drizzle in the oil while whisking or blending. When all of the oil has been added, taste and season.

Please note: mayonnaise only curdles if the oil is added too quickly at the beginning. If that happens, don't worry. All you need to do is put a fresh egg yolk into a clean bowl, add the curdled mixture to it, drop by drop, whisking continuously. Continue adding the rest of the oil.

For The Apple, Watermelon And Hazelnut Salad

Combine all the ingredients just before serving.

To Serve

Break the salmon into pieces and arrange on 4 plates with the apple, cucumber, watermelon and hazelnut salad. Dot the saffron mayonnaise around the plates.

Chef's Tip

I would always recommend curing and smoking your own salmon however, if you are pushed for time, you can always ask your local fishmonger to buy some in for you.

ROASTED LEG OF CHICKEN WITH PUY LENTILS

SERVES 4

 *Pinot Noir, 2012, The Crusher, California (USA)*

Ingredients

Chicken

4 chicken legs
½ bunch thyme
½ bulb garlic (skin on)
2 bay leaves
200ml rapeseed oil

Puy Lentils

150g puy lentils
300ml good quality chicken stock
1 bay leaf
3 sprigs thyme
1 carrot (finely diced)
1 small leek (white of, finely diced)
1 stick celery (finely diced)
15g butter
salt (pinch of)
double cream (splash of)

Method

For The Chicken (Prepare ahead)

Preheat the oven to 120°C (fan).

Cover the chicken legs, thyme, garlic and bay leaves with the oil in a deep baking tray. Place greaseproof paper over the tray and wrap tin foil around the whole tray. Transfer to the oven for 2 hours. Leave to cool.

Once cooled, cover the tray with cling film and store in the fridge until ready to use.

Chef's Tip

The *confit* process can be done up to 3 days in advance. You can cover the chicken legs with the oil, *confit* them in the oven and they can be stored, covered in the oil and wrapped well with cling film and kept in the fridge until they are needed. The longer the chicken legs have to sit in the fat, the more succulent they will be.

For The Puy Lentils

Soak the lentils for 1 hour in cold water, then give them a good rinse. Simmer the lentils, chicken stock, bay leaf and thyme in a pot for 20 minutes or until the lentils are tender. Remove the bay leaf and the thyme and keep the lentils warm.

Melt the butter in a separate pan and sweat the carrot, leek and celery until tender. While the vegetables are still warm, stir them into the lentils with a splash of cream. The stock and the cream will create a sauce for the lentils

To Serve

Preheat the oven to 180°C.

Take the chicken legs out of the oil and place them in a non-stick pan, skin-side down. Place the pan in the oven for 20 minutes. The skin will crisp up, but the meat will remain amazingly soft and tender. Warm the lentils through and serve a generous spoonful of the lentils topped with a chicken leg on each plate.

(see glossary)

TREACLE TART, HONEYCOMB & VANILLA CREAM

SERVES 8

Pedro Ximénez 'Triana', Bodegas Hidalgo, Jerez (Spain)

Ingredients

Treacle Tart

180g brown bread (crusts removed, roughly torn)
85g unsalted butter
3 medium free-range eggs
75ml double cream
9g salt
750g golden syrup

Honeycomb

315g caster sugar
125g liquid glucose
50g honey
60ml water
15g bicarbonate of soda
butter (for greasing)

Vanilla Cream

200ml double cream
2 tbsp icing sugar
½ vanilla pod (seeds of)

23cm tart tin (lined with greaseproof paper)
20cm square tin

Method

For The Treacle Tart

Preheat the oven to 180°C (fan).

Place the bread in a food processor and pulse to fine breadcrumbs.

Heat the butter in a pan until browned, then strain through a fine sieve into a bowl, leaving the sediment behind.

Mix the eggs, cream and salt in a bowl until well combined.

Gently heat the golden syrup in a pan and stir in the strained butter. Pour the syrup mixture into the egg and cream mixture and stir in the breadcrumbs.

Pour the mixture into the prepared tin and bake in the oven for 25 minutes.

Turn the oven temperature down to 140°C (fan) and bake for a further 20 minutes, or until the tart is golden brown and bubbling. Remove from the oven and allow to cool, before turning out and cutting into slices.

For The Honeycomb

Grease the square tin with the butter.

Mix the sugar, liquid glucose, honey and water in a pan and stir over a gentle heat until the sugar has melted. Once completely melted, turn up the heat a little and simmer until you have an amber coloured caramel, or until it reaches 147°C on a sugar thermometer. Turn off the heat, tip in the bicarbonate and beat in with a wooden spoon until it has all disappeared and the mixture is foaming. Scrape into the tin immediately, but be careful as the mixture will be hot and will continue bubbling. Leave it to set for about 1 hour. The honeycomb will then be ready to snap into chunks.

For The Vanilla Cream

Whip all of the ingredients together until the cream forms soft peaks.

To Serve

Serve each slice of the tart with a spoonful of the vanilla cream and a few pieces of honeycomb. At Bistro Moderne, we serve the treacle tart with pecan lollipops and sugar puff tuile. These are optional but delicious extras.

Chef's Tip

This treacle tart freezes extremely well due to the fact that there is no pastry on it. Take it out of the freezer about 2 hours before serving.

068 BLACKADDIE HOUSE HOTEL

Blackaddie Road, Sanquhar, Dumfriesshire, DG4 6JJ

01659 50270
www.blackaddiehotel.co.uk Twitter: @blackaddie

Food, service and genuinely warm hospitality are at the very heart of what Blackaddie is all about. The food is outstanding - don't just take our word for it, one look at the guest book will confirm this.

Owned by Ian and Jane McAndrew, Blackaddie has been setting enviable standards since they bought the hotel in 2007. Ian, formerly the youngest Englishman to be awarded a Michelin Star, presides over the kitchens where absolutely everything is made in house from the finest of ingredients, many of which are either local, or closer still, from their own kitchen garden.

Jane oversees the front of house ensuring that guests feel at home from the moment they arrive. Together they've made Blackaddie a renowned destination in what is a beautiful, yet little known area of Scotland.

Situated only 45 miles from Glasgow and within easy reach of Edinburgh, 30 miles from Ayr and Dumfries, it is a 'must try' destination. With some lovely rooms, one with a super king size 4 poster and many with jacuzzi style baths, the hotel offers peace and tranquillity alongside an unforgettable dining experience and is the perfect spot for a romantic getaway or celebration, or even for just a few days of comfort and indulgence in style.

Blackaddie photography: Robin Stewart www.realfoodphotography.co

Ian has a string of accolades, not only for Blackaddie, but over many years for his previous restaurants. Many top chefs have been through his hands, including Andrew Fairlie, Paul Kitching, Michael Dean and Phil Vickery. Ian is now in the kitchens of Blackaddie, working with his small team, to bring his own distinctive style of food to south west Scotland.

SEARED SCALLOPS WITH TASTES & TEXTURES OF CAULIFLOWER

SERVES 4

Either a rich Viognier or fragrant Gewürztraminer

Ingredients

Seared Scallops

8 diver caught scallops (out of the shell)
50ml olive oil, seasoning

Curried Cauliflower

150g cauliflower (cut into florets)
50ml olive oil or ghee
30g shallot (finely chopped)
10g fresh ginger (fine julienne)
10g garlic (crushed)
½ red chilli (de-seeded, finely chopped)
2g cumin seeds
4g Madras curry powder
3g garam masala
1 Cox apple (peeled, cut into 1cm dice)
20g raisins
salt and freshly ground pepper (to season)
10g flaked almonds (toasted)
5g fresh coriander leaf (chopped)

Cauliflower Purée

180g cauliflower (roughly chopped)
70g potato (peeled, roughly chopped)
25g shallot (roughly chopped)
5g garlic (roughly chopped)
50ml double cream
100ml milk, seasoning

Crushed Cauliflower

180g cauliflower
25g unsalted butter, seasoning

Cauliflower Tempura

12 tight, small cauliflower florets
90g flour, 20g cornflour
½ tsp bicarbonate of soda
240ml water, seasoning

Garnish

coriander leaf (chopped)

Method

For The Curried Cauliflower

Heat the olive oil and gently fry the shallots, ginger, garlic, chillies and cumin seeds for 1 minute without browning. Stir in the curry powder and the garam masala. Gently fry for a further minute. Add the cauliflower florets and the apple along with the raisins and about 100ml water. Season and cook over a brisk heat, stirring often, until the cauliflower is just cooked. Remove from the heat and cool.

For The Cauliflower Purée

Place all the ingredients in a saucepan, season lightly and cover with tin foil and a tight fitting lid. Bring to the boil, then either simmer very slowly on the hob, or place in an oven at about 150°C until the cauliflower and potato are fully cooked. Blend in a food processor until very smooth.

For The Crushed Cauliflower

Cook the cauliflower in boiling, salted water until slightly *al dente*. Refresh, drain and crush.

For The Cauliflower Tempura

Make up a tempura batter using all the ingredients. Lightly flour the florets and dip into the batter.

To Sear The Scallops

Heat the olive oil in a frying pan until very hot. Season the scallops and sear them in the hot pan, browning well on both sides until cooked.

To Finish And Serve

Deep fry the tempura cauliflower. Stir the coriander and flaked almonds through the curried cauliflower. Reheat the cauliflower purée and reheat the crushed cauliflower in the butter.

Place 2 spoons of crushed cauliflower on each plate and top each with a seared scallop. Put 2 swipes of purée on each plate and spoon the curried cauliflower onto these. Decorate with 3 tempura cauliflower per plate. Scatter with coriander leaves.

Chef's Tip

One cauliflower, weighing 500g, should be plenty to make this dish. Break the cauliflower into nice shaped florets for the tempura and save the rest for the other elements of the dish.

PAN ROAST SEA BASS WITH ROAST SALSIFY, NEW POTATOES, SPINACH & BABY ONIONS, PUY LENTIL JUS

SERVES 4

Try a light red such as Pinot Noir, possibly from Chile

Ingredients

Sea Bass

4 x 150g portions sea bass (scaled)
40ml olive oil
salt and freshly ground white pepper

Salsify

350g salsify (peeled)
30g flour, 1 litre water
1 lemon, 12g salt, 4g sugar
20ml oil, 40g butter

Puy Lentils

40g puy lentils (rinsed)
1 shallot (peeled), 2 cloves garlic
1/4 stick celery, 150ml veal jus

New Potatoes

320g new potatoes (peeled)
50g butter, seasoning

Baby Onions

20 baby onions (peeled)
20ml olive oil, 20g butter

Spinach

175g fresh leaf spinach (washed, stalks removed, wilted in 20g butter, seasoned)

Chef's Tip

While many chefs use butter to cook their fish, I do not as I prefer to use only a light olive oil. This leaves the fish tasting cleaner and does not complicate the flavour. When cooking the fish, it is important to make sure the pan is hot enough so the fish browns and crisps. If it is too cool, the fish will boil instead.

Method

For Salsify

Cut the salsify into 10cm lengths, allowing for 4 lengths per portion. If the salsify is quite thick then, once cooked, cut the thick pieces in half lengthways. Squeeze the lemon juice into the water and whisk in the flour. Add the lemon shell, the salt and the sugar. Plunge the salsify into this and bring to the boil, stirring often to prevent the flour from sitting on the bottom of the pan and burning. Simmer until the salsify is just cooked. Remove from the heat and cool. Wash the salsify and dry. When ready to serve, heat the oil in a frying pan and, when hot, add the butter. When sizzling, add the salsify, season and fry gently until lightly brown. Drain and keep warm.

For The Puy Lentils

Place the lentils in a pan with the shallot, garlic and celery. Cover well with water, bring to the boil and simmer until just cooked. Drain and cool. Discard the vegetables. Heat the veal jus with the drained lentils.

For The New Potatoes

Cook the potatoes in boiling, salted water. Drain and roughly crush. Set aside. To serve, warm the potatoes with the butter and season as necessary.

For The Baby Onions

Blanch the baby onions in boiling, salted water until half cooked. Drain and cool. Heat the oil and butter in a frying pan, season and fry the onions until lightly browned. Drain and keep warm.

For The Sea Bass

Season the sea bass on both sides. Heat the olive oil in a frying pan, and when hot, place the fish in, skin-side down. Fry until golden, then turn over. Remove the pan from the heat, but leave the fish in the pan. Keep warm.

To Serve

Place a pile of the crushed potatoes in the centre of the plate. Arrange 4 pieces of salsify on the potato and a piece of fish on top of the salsify. Divide the spinach to allow 5 small piles per plate around the fish. Top each one of these with an onion and spoon the lentils around.

(see glossary)

ICED LEMON POSSET PARFAIT WITH RASPBERRIES, MERINGUE & PISTACHIO CAKE

SERVES 10

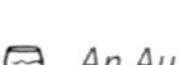

An Australian sticky Chardonnay, such as Stump Jump.

Ingredients

Iced Lemon Posset Parfait

575ml double cream
215g caster sugar
3 lemons (juice of, rinds reserved)
3 medium eggs (2 separated)

Raspberry Coulis

125g raspberries (washed)
50g caster sugar
½ lemon (juice of)

Meringues

50g egg whites, 100g caster sugar
1 lemon (fine zest of), 5g fennel powder

Pistachio Cake

25g polenta flour
100g pistachio paste
25g plain flour, ½ tsp baking powder
60ml olive oil
50g unsalted butter (melted, cooled)
2 medium eggs
100g caster sugar
½ orange (juice of)
½ lemon (juice and grated zest of)

Honeycomb

120g white sugar
40g golden syrup
50ml water
1 tsp bicarbonate of soda

Garnish

candied lemon zest

32cm x 21cm x 4cm cake tin (lined)
cake tin (lined with greaseproof paper)
terrine mould

Method

For The Iced Lemon Posset Parfait

Boil 450ml of cream with 125g sugar for 2-3 minutes. Mix in the lemon juice. Cover and leave to go cold.

Combine 50g of sugar with 50g egg white over a *bain-marie*. Whisk until it reaches 38°C. Remove from the heat and whisk until cold. Whip the remaining cream to soft peaks.

Combine the egg and yolks with 40g of sugar and whisk over a *bain-marie* to 70°C. Remove from the heat and whisk until cold.

Gently fold the posset into the egg mix, then fold in the meringue and whipped cream until completely mixed through and smooth.

Set in the freezer in tubes made from acetate, or in rings, or even in a terrine mould, for 3 hours.

For The Raspberry Coulis

Heat the ingredients until the raspberries start to bubble. Blitz until smooth and pass through a fine sieve. Leave to cool.

For The Meringues

Whisk the egg whites and sugar in a *bain-marie* until it reaches 38°C. Remove from the heat and whisk until cold.

Zest the lemon over the mix, then spoon hazelnut-size spoons onto parchment paper. Dust with fennel powder and dry in an oven on its coolest setting until crisp on the outside, but a little soft in the centre.

For The Pistachio Cake

Preheat the oven to 160°C.

Combine the dry ingredients with the pistachio paste. Add the oil to the butter. Whisk the eggs and sugar until pale, then slowly whisk in the fats, followed by the pistachio mix, citrus juice and zest. Transfer this very wet mixture (it will work!) to the tin. Bake for 50 minutes. Cool for 10 minutes before removing from the tin.

For The Honeycomb

Stir the sugar, syrup and water over a gentle heat in a pan. Once the sugar has dissolved, boil for 7 minutes. Remove from the heat and quickly add the bicarbonate of soda. Stir quickly while it froths and pour into the prepared tin. Cool. When cold, break into pieces.

To Serve

Garnish with candied lemon zest and serve as pictured.

Chef's Tip

You can prepare all elements of this dish ahead.

(see glossary)

MICHELIN STAR SPOTLIGHT...

COLIN CRAIG & LESLEY CROSFIELD

CHEF & PROPRIETORS, THE ALBANNACH

As self-taught chef and proprietors, it's staggering to believe that we are now entering our 25th year at The Albannach, which has held a Michelin star since 2009. The hotel's five rooms and luxurious suites are largely the result of winters spent renovating with respect for the charm and integrity of this old Highland house.

Since 1990 we have sourced the wonderful natural larder of the far north west of the Scottish coastline and more recently, since acquiring the four acre croft surrounding The Albannach, we have been developing the production of some of our own vegetables, herbs and fruit in our polytunnel and fruit cages. We are excited that the summer of 2015 will see the arrival of a hive or two of bees, with pollination the priority. Two local crofters have long provided eggs, flowers, jam and organic vegetables. Shellfish land at The Albannach's door daily, and wild sea fish caught locally are readily available. Free-range farm produce and game come from old friends - The Gibsons at Macbeth's in Forres, Morayshire.

Lochinver, a working harbour town, nestles in a deep sea loch at the foot of two spectacular yet accessible peaks; Suilven, 'the Sugar Loaf' and Canisp. Each fulfils a day's walk from the hotel and are visible from The Albannach's conservatory, terrace and garden (which now boasts a midge-eating machine!). We will happily share our local knowledge of the scenic, meandering mountains, both of which will take your breath away. Boat trips to islands are also locally available.

Regarded by many as 'Europe's last wilderness', this empty corner of the north west Highlands soothes the urban soul, and what better way to celebrate this stunning area than with a stay at The Albannach. We look forward to welcoming you.

The Albannach Hotel, Baddidarroch, Lochinver, Sutherland, IV27 4LP.
01571 844 407 www.thealbannach.co.uk

080
THE CELLAR RESTAURANT

24 East Green, Anstruther, Fife, Scotland, KY10 3AA

01333 310 378
www.thecellaranstruther.co.uk Twitter: @billy_boyter Facebook: The Cellar Anstruther

For more than 40 years, The Cellar has been a leading restaurant in the East Neuk of Fife. It reopened its doors in April 2014 under the ownership of chef Billy Boyter and his family, assisted by the restaurant manager Patricia Kirk.

One of the new generations of talented and exciting chefs, Billy, who is originally from Anstruther, has spent the last 16 years learning his trade in some of Scotland's best restaurants. He has also represented Scotland numerous times throughout his career, notably winning The World Junior Masterchef Challenge in New Zealand and also The World Culinary Cup in Luxembourg in 2002.

Over the centuries the building has had a rich history; a smokehouse, cooperage and even a store for fishermen's gear. The Cellar respects that heritage and also its place in a region rich in amazing, raw ingredients. Using the best of produce from local suppliers whenever possible, The Cellar offers great Scottish food served in a unique and beautiful restaurant. Complementing the food is their impressive selection of locally produced beers, Scottish gins, whisky and carefully selected wines from around the world.

The Cellar
The Cellar Restaurant
24

With a kitchen team consisting of just Billy Boyter and one other, keeping the food simple is key.
"Using quality seasonal ingredients cooked properly is our way of thinking," says Billy.

KILDUNCAN DUCK EGG, NORTH SEA COD, CAULIFLOWER & SMOKED MAYONNAISE

SERVES 4

 *Chablis, Domaine Bernard Defaix 2013 (France)*

Ingredients

4 duck eggs

Cured Cod

400g cod fillet
1 lemon (zest of)
sea salt

Cauliflower Purée

1 cauliflower
50g butter
1 clove garlic (crushed)
½ lemon (juice and zest of)
2g squid ink

Smoked Mayonnaise

2 duck yolks
5ml cider vinegar
160ml pomace oil
salt
pepper

Garnish

Pepper Dulse seaweed
shaved cauliflower
rapeseed oil
sea purslane

Method

For The Cured Cod

Firstly skin the cod, reserving the skin for later. Trim off any brown meat from the fillet and heavily season with the sea salt and zest. Leave in the salt for 1 hour. Wash the cod, pat dry and roll in cling film to achieve a cylinder shape. Poach in a water bath at 50°C for 1 hour, then slice just before serving. Alternatively, poach in gently simmering water.

Scrape back the cod skin and dehydrate in a low oven (90°C fan) until dry, for about 1-1½ hours. Once dry, cut into strips and fry at 170°C until crisp.

For The Cauliflower Purée

Thinly slice the cauliflower (we use a *mandolin* slicer) and add to a pot of boiling, seasoned water. Quickly cook until tender. Make a *beurre noisette* with the butter, garlic and lemon. Strain the cauliflower from the water and blend until completely smooth, adding in the noisette as it is blitzing. Finally add in the squid ink and check the seasoning.

For The Smoked Mayonnaise

Whisk the yolks and vinegar together in a bowl with a pinch of salt and pepper. While continuously whisking, slowly add in the oil until you have a thick mayonnaise (if it's too thick, just add a touch of water). Cover the bowl with cling film and, using a hand held smoker, fill the bowl with smoke (we use applewood wood chips) and leave for 30 minutes.

For The Duck Egg

Poach the duck egg at 64°C for 1 hour. Remove from the water bath and gently remove from the shell.

To Serve

Season the egg with salt and the Pepper Dulse seaweed.
Place some of the smoked mayonnaise in the centre of the plate and gently lay on the duck egg. Slice the cured and poached cod and arrange around the egg. Add a few dots of the cauliflower purée and finish with the cauliflower slices dressed in the rapeseed oil and the sea purslane leaves.

Chef's Tip

Source the best quality cod that you can and always try to source local, fresh duck eggs.

(see glossary)

SEGGIE & DATE GLAZED DUCK, HERITAGE CARROTS, PARMESAN POLENTA, PICKLED PEAR

SERVES 4

Zephyr, Marlborough, Pinot Noir 2011 (New Zealand)

Ingredients

2 male duck breasts (trimmed, skin scored in a criss-cross pattern, seasoned)

Parmesan Polenta

500ml full-fat milk, 30g butter
175g fine ground polenta
40g Parmesan (finely grated)
2 egg yolks, seasoning

Carrot Purée

500g heritage or organic carrots (peeled)
40g butter, salt

Confit Carrots

4 medium heritage carrots (gently scrubbed, tops intact)
2 star anise, 30g butter, 1 sprig lemon thyme, salt

Seggie Porter And Date Glaze

330ml Seggie Porter (or similar style beer)
75g honey, 100g dates
50ml Chardonnay vinegar, 15g brown sauce, salt

Pickled Pear

1 ripe pear, 100ml water
50ml Chardonnay vinegar
2g allspice berries, 1 fresh bay leaf
25g sugar, 1g salt

Duck Sauce

200g duck trimmings, 50g smoked bacon (diced)
80g carrots (diced), 180g shallots (shredded)
2 cloves garlic (crushed)
40ml Cabernet Sauvignon vinegar
400ml Pinot Noir, 1½ litres duck stock

Garnish

baby onions (caramelised)
carrot crumb, nasturtium leaves

Method

For The Parmesan Polenta

Bring the milk and butter to the boil and rain in the polenta, whisking constantly. Take off the heat and mix in the Parmesan, followed by the yolks. Check the seasoning, then roll out the polenta between 2 layers of cling film and leave to set in the fridge for 30 minutes. Once set, cut into 2cm x 15cm fingers. Pan fry both sides until golden to finish.

For The Carrot Purée

Cook all the ingredients in a vac pack in a water bath, or steamer, at 90°C until tender. Blitz until smooth. Season and pass through a fine sieve.

For The Confit Carrot

Keep the carrot frills from the tops for garnishing. Combine with the other ingredients and seal in a vacuum bag. Cook in a water bath at 86°C for around 2 hours, depending on the size of the carrots. Once ready, remove from the bag and colour in a pan with foaming butter to finish. Alternatively, slow roast the carrots (120°C fan) for about 2 hours.

For The Seggie Porter And Date Glaze

Bring all the ingredients to the boil, then purée until smooth with a hand blender. Reduce until thickened.

For The Pickled Pear

Slice 4 pieces of pear, about 1cm thick, and cut them out with a circle cutter. Combine the pickle ingredients and bring to the boil. Leave to cool slightly, then pour the hot mixture over the pear slices. Leave to cool to room temperature.

For The Duck Sauce

Colour the bacon and trimmings in a little oil. Remove from the pot, then colour the carrots. Add the shallots and garlic, reduce the heat and sweat down until soft. Add the meat back in and *deglaze* with the vinegar. Add the wine and reduce to almost nothing. Add the stock and reduce, skimming the sauce until the correct consistency is reached. Pass through a muslin cloth.

For The Duck Breasts

Lay the breasts skin-side down in a hot pan, ensuring the skin is in full contact with the pan. When the skin has coloured and rendered down, turn the breasts and cook for 3-4 minutes. Remove from the pan and rest for 4 minutes. Brush with the glaze and carve into 4.

To Serve

Serve as pictured.

(see glossary)

CHOCOLATE CUSTARD, BLOOD ORANGE CURD, BUTTERMILK & COCONUT SORBET

SERVES 4

Beerenauslese, Domäne Wachau, 2013 (Austria)

Ingredients

Set Chocolate Custard

200ml milk
50ml double cream
50g sugar
100g yolks (5-6 eggs)
2 sheets gelatine (soaked in cold water)
255g Valrhona orange noir chocolate

Blood Orange Curd

100ml water
100g sugar
2 blood oranges (juice and zest of)
salt (pinch of)
50g butter (melted)
15g ultratex (approximately)

Hazelnut Sponge

65g roasted ground hazelnuts
20g plain flour
25g praline
85g egg white (2-3 eggs)
65g yolk (2-3 eggs)
30g sugar

Buttermilk And Coconut Sorbet

600ml buttermilk
250g coconut purée
150g sugar
1 leaf gelatine (soaked in cold water)

Garnish

lemon balm leaves
chocolate biscuits (crumbled)
orange powder

5cm square moulds
gas canister (1 charge)

Method

For Set Chocolate Custard

Mix the cream and milk together and bring to the boil. Whisk the sugar and yolks, then pour the hot milk slowly into it, mixing all the time. Return to the stove and cook to 83°C. Stir in the gelatine. Strain the mixture over the chocolate and rest for a minute to let the chocolate melt. *Emulsify* together with a hand blender while cooling. Pipe into square moulds and leave to set.

For The Blood Orange Curd

Make a syrup with the sugar and water and leave to cool slightly. Once cooled, add the blood orange juice, zest, a pinch of salt and melted butter. Blend together, adding a little ultratex at a time until the correct consistency is reached. Place in a piping bag.

Chef's Tip

We make an eggless curd for this dish. This method gives a much fresher, lighter curd. If you don't have any of these ingredients, a regular lime curd recipe will work just fine.

For The Hazelnut Sponge

Blend all the ingredients together and pour into a CO_2 gas canister. Charge with 1 gas capsule and leave to rest for 1 hour. Discharge into a disposable cup and microwave on full power for 45 seconds. Once cool, remove the sponge from the cup and gently tear into small pieces.

For The Buttermilk And Coconut Sorbet

Place all ingredients in a pot and warm together on the stove. Churn in an ice cream machine until ready.

To Serve

De-mould the custard onto the plate and add a few dots of the blood orange curd on top. Place on the hazelnut sponge and a few lemon balm leaves. Using a metal ring, form a circular shape of chocolate biscuit crumbs, then position a scoop of buttermilk sorbet on top.

(see glossary)

090
THE COURTYARD

1 Alford Lane, Aberdeen, AB10 1YD

01224 589 109
www.thecourtyardaberdeen.co.uk Twitter: @foodiebeetroot

The Courtyard is a hidden gem in the west end of Aberdeen, tucked away in a leafy lane just off the main thoroughfare. The Courtyard is a welcoming dining experience for those in the know, as well as those who stumble upon it.

A perfect combination of a relaxed atmosphere; fresh, local, seasonal ingredients and the creative flair of the culinary team provide diners with a feast for all the senses.

At the helm of this culinary journey is the executive chef and owner Chris Tonner, head chef Ross Cochrane and general manager Carolina Carleschi. Their joint skills come together seamlessly to ensure that first class food, service, and dining experience are given to every guest, both in The Courtyard and at sister restaurant The Adelphi Kitchen - which is Aberdeen's flagship, charcoal cooked meat and seafood restaurant.

The Courtyard brings to your plate the best of Scottish seasonal produce, cooked well and presented beautifully to give you not only a taste sensation but also a visual delight. Chris and Ross take their time to explore and source their ingredients from local suppliers to ensure that you get the freshest produce, from trusted suppliers, as close to the restaurant as possible.

Come and experience what The Courtyard has to offer. We promise your first visit won't be your last!

The Courtyard is an integral cog in the Beetroot Restaurants' machine. They have won various awards and the highlight so far is an AA Rosette at their sister restaurant The Adelphi Kitchen.
The team work together seamlessly to ensure that the service complements the food perfectly.

Courtyard

SEARED GROUSE, TEXTURES OF BEETROOT, SAFFRON, POACHED PEAR, GOAT'S CHEESE PANNA COTTA, CANDIED WALNUTS

SERVES 4

White: Lolo Albariño (Spain)
Red: Angus the Bull Cabernet Sauvignon (Australia)

Ingredients

2-3 grouse (size dependent)

Beetroot

3 purple beets
3 golden beets
75ml vinegar
125g sugar
50ml water
½ tsp agar agar

Poached Pears

2 Conference pears (peeled)
200ml white wine
200g sugar
saffron (pinch of)

Goat's Cheese Panna Cotta

100g goat's cheese
100ml milk
100ml cream
2-3 sheets gelatine (soaked in cold water)

Candied Walnuts

50g sugar
10ml water
50g butter (chilled, diced)
50g walnuts

4 moulds (8cm wide x 2cm deep)

Chef's Tip

When adding the gelatine, make sure the panna cotta is below 70°C.

Method

For The Textures Of Beetroot

Peel one of each beetroot, cut into small dice and keep separate. Make a small batch of pickling liquor by combining the vinegar, sugar and water. Whisk together until the sugar dissolves. Split between two small pans, add the diced beetroot, bring to the boil and set the pans aside.

Preheat the oven to 140°C (fan).

Roast one of each beetroot in the oven for 45 minutes until soft. Peel whilst still warm and cut into wedges. Set aside.

Peel and grate the 2 remaining beetroots and sweat in a pan for 3-4 minutes. Add enough water to cover the beetroot, then cook for 20-25 minutes until soft.

Blitz the cooked beetroot in a blender, add the agar agar, then pass through a fine sieve. Set aside.

For The Poached Pears

Bring the sugar, white wine and a pinch of saffron to the boil. Add the peeled pears and cook for about 10-15 minutes until soft, then set aside to cool. When chilled, remove the cores and cut into quarters.

For The Goat's Cheese Panna Cotta

Bring the goat's cheese, milk and cream to the boil and simmer for 5-10 minutes. Stir the gelatine into the mixture, then blitz the ingredients in a blender. Pass through a fine sieve.
Mix thoroughly, then pour into moulds. Leave to set in the fridge for 2-3 hours.

For The Candied Walnuts

In a heavy bottomed pan, add the sugar and water and bring to the boil. Keep a close eye on this. When the sugar becomes a light brown colour, slowly add the butter, a cube at a time. When the butter has been completely incorporated, add the walnuts and shake for about 1-2 minutes. Pour onto greaseproof paper and leave to cool.

For The Grouse

Preheat the oven to 180°C (fan).

Pan sear the whole grouse then place in the oven for 6-8 minutes. Remove from bone and serve pink.

To Serve

Serve as pictured.

RABBIT SADDLE WITH WILD MUSHROOM MOUSSE & CONFIT RABBIT LEG

SERVES 4

White: Stoneburn Sauvignon Blanc (New Zealand)
Red: Featherdrop Hill Pinot Noir (New Zealand)

Ingredients

1 whole rabbit (back legs removed and saddle deboned)

Confit Rabbit Legs

1 lemon (zest of)
4 cardamom pods
1 tsp white peppercorns
1 tbsp fleur de sel
10g sugar
3 carrots (*brunoise*)
1 stick celery (*brunoise*)
10 banana shallots (*brunoise*)
1 garlic bulb (cut in half)
duck fat (to cover)
150ml Madeira wine, 500ml beef jus

Herb Breadcrumb

100g panko (Japanese breadcrumbs)
2 tbsp flat leaf parsley (chopped)
2 sprigs lemon thyme (picked)
1 tbsp extra virgin olive oil
beaten egg and flour (to *panné*)

Wild Mushroom And Chicken Mousse

150g chicken
20g egg yolk
10g salt
350ml double cream
150g wild mushrooms (preferably foraged-fresh, chopped)
1 tbsp truffle oil, 2 shallots (*brunoise*)

Mushroom Purée

1 banana shallot (finely diced)
50g unsalted butter
150g mixed wild mushrooms (chopped)
15ml white truffle oil
100ml white wine
salt and pepper (to season)

To Serve

baby vegetables (carrot, leek, navet)

Method

For The Confit Rabbit Legs (Prepare ahead)

Rub the legs with lemon zest, cardamom pods, white peppercorns, fleur de sel and sugar and marinate for 8 hours.

Rinse under cold running water, pat dry and place in the duck fat. *Confit* at 100°C (fan) for 8 hours. Let the rabbit come to room temperature in the fat, then remove and wipe off any excess oil. Pick the meat from the bones, making sure to remove all bones - reserve some bones to make the lollipops.

Sauté the vegetables and garlic until lightly coloured. *Deglaze* the pan with the Madeira, then add the jus. Bring to the boil, reduce, then remove from the heat and allow to come to room temperature. Combine the stock with the picked meat, then roll into balls. Place a trimmed bone in the ball forming a lollipop. Place in the fridge for 2-3 hours to solidify.

For The Herb Breadcrumb

Place the ingredients in a mixer to produce fine crumbs.
Once the lollipops have firmed, roll in the flour, beaten egg and finally in the herb breadcrumb.

For The Wild Mushroom And Chicken Mousse

Blitz the chicken, yolk and salt in a processor, then slowly add the cream. Carefully pour through a fine sieve.

Sweat the wild mushrooms with the shallots in a little truffle oil. Cool, then stir into the chicken mousse.

Chef's Tip

When making the chicken mousse, add the cream in 3 stages, keeping the blender in the fridge between blitzing. Keep under 5°C to stop the mix splitting.

For The Rabbit Saddle

Lay the rabbit fillet on cling film and pipe the mousse alongside. Roll tightly. Place in a vacuum bag and cook at 67½°C in a water bath for 12 hours. Remove and place in ice water. Alternatively, steam at 60°C for 1½ hours.

For The Mushroom Purée

Sweat the shallot in the butter, then add the wild mushrooms. Cook for around 5 minutes, then add the white wine and truffle oil. Cook until most of the wine has evaporated. Purée until smooth, season and keep warm.

To Serve

Cover the rabbit saddle with tin foil and place in the oven (180°C fan) for 6-8 minutes. Deep fry the lollipops at 140°C for around 6 minutes until golden and crisp.

Remove the tin foil and pan fry the saddle until golden brown. Carve and present as pictured.

(see glossary)

LEMON CUSTARD TART, EARL GREY CREAM, ORANGE GEL, LIME & ELDERFLOWER SORBET, MADELEINES

SERVES 4

White: Moscato dessert wine (Italy)
Red dessert wine: Banyuls Red dessert wine (France)

Ingredients

Pastry

125g butter
250g flour, 1 egg
90g sugar, salt (pinch of)
1 egg yolk (to egg wash)

Lemon Custard Mix

175ml lemon juice, 100ml double cream
3 egg yolks, 125g sugar

Earl Grey Cream

325ml double cream, 110ml milk
4 Earl Grey teabags, 65g sugar
3 leaves gelatine (soaked in cold water)

Orange Gel

1 whole orange (peel and juice of)
10g ultratex, 100g sugar

Lime And Elderflower Sorbet

250ml water
2 limes (juice and zest of)
100ml elderflower cordial
200g caster sugar
3 tbsp liquid glucose

Madeleines

1 egg, 50g flour
50g butter, 50g sugar
½ tsp baking powder

4 individual tart cases
4 small rectangular or square moulds
Madeleine moulds

Chef's Tip

Once your pastry is rolled and in the tart case, place back in the fridge for 15-20 minutes. This will help the pastry to stay stable when cooking.

Method

For The Pastry

Bind all the ingredients (except the egg yolk) together, roll and knead into a dough. Leave to rest in the fridge for 30-45 minutes. Bring to room temperature and roll to 12-14cm diameter (2-3mm thick).

Preheat the oven to 160°C (fan).

Line the tart cases with the pastry and blind bake for 6-8 minutes. Remove the baking beans, seal with egg yolk and bake for 2-3 minutes. Leave to cool.

For The Lemon Custard Mix

Reduce the lemon juice to 120ml, add the double cream and bring to the boil. Whisk the eggs and sugar together, then pour in the warm liquid. Pass through a fine sieve and leave to chill for 1 hour. Pour into the tart cases and bake at 120°C (fan) for 20-30 minutes. Turn the oven off and leave the tarts in the oven until the mix has set. Serve lightly chilled.

For The Earl Grey Cream

Bring the milk, cream and teabags to the boil. Simmer for 8-10 minutes on a low heat. Squeeze the excess water from the gelatine and add to the hot mix with the sugar. Pass through a fine sieve and pour into the 4 moulds. Leave to set for 2-3 hours in the fridge.

For The Orange Gel

Peel the orange and put the peel in a pan. Cover with cold water and bring to the boil. Reduce the water until the pan is almost dry, then refresh in cold water. Repeat this process 4 times.
On the last reduction, add the peel to a blender and use juice from the orange to make into a purée. (You may need some water to thin this down). Add the ultratex until a gel like consistency is reached. Add sugar to taste.

For The Lime And Elderflower Sorbet

Bring the water to the boil, add the lime juice and zest, elderflower cordial, liquid glucose and the sugar. Heat to 82°C, then leave to cool. Churn for 25 minutes in an ice cream machine.

For The Madeleines

Preheat the oven to 150°C (fan).

Combine all the ingredients and pipe into Madeleine moulds. Bake for 10-12 minutes.

To Serve

Serve as pictured.

100

CRAIG MILLAR @16 WEST END

16 West End, St Monans, Fife, KY10 2BX

01333 730 327
www.16westend.com Twitter: @craigcmillar

Born and educated in Dundee, Craig Millar started his career with Crest Hotels in Buckinghamshire before moving back north of the border, working in several restaurants and hotels. Among them was Murrayshall House Hotel, under the guidance of Bruce Sangster. In 1998 Craig joined up with Tim Butler for what was to be a 13 year partnership at The Seafood Restaurant in St Monans and they went on to open The Seafood Restaurant, St Andrews, in 2003. It was during this period that the pair won accolades such as SLTN Restaurant of the Year, AA Restaurant of the Year, AA Wine List of the Year, AA Seafood Restaurant of the Year, CIS Restaurant of the Year, Scottish Restaurant Awards 'Speciality Restaurant of the Year'. Both restaurants were also named 'Newcomer of the Year' in the Good Food Guide. Craig was also named 'Seafood Restaurant Chef of the Year' and he won 'Taste of Scotland Lamb Challenge'.

After a major renovation in June 2011, Craig took sole ownership of the St Monans Restaurant, renaming it Craig Millar @ 16 West End.

Within the first eight months, the restaurant picked up CIS Newcomer of the Year. The menu now includes more meat and game dishes rather than just specialising in seafood, and Craig champions the use of local produce.

The restaurant occupies an old fisherman's cottage and features an 800-year-old freshwater well with mythical, healing powers. There is an open fire in the Victorian style lounge where pre-dinner or after-dinner drinks can be enjoyed and an outside terrace to use during the warmer weather. Picture windows in the restaurant's modern extension allow diners to admire views of the harbour.

Craig
Millar
16 West End
@

The restaurant currently holds 2 AA Rosettes, a rating of 5 in The Good Food Guide, Winner of Newcomer of the Year 2012 CIS Excellence Awards and Finalist Restaurant of the Year 2014 CIS Excellence Awards.

PEA MOUSSE, PICKLED SHALLOTS & MUSHROOMS

SERVES 6-8

Petit Clos, Clos Henri, Sauvignon Blanc, 2013 (New Zealand)

Ingredients

Pea Mousse

250g peas
250ml whipping cream
1½ sheets gelatine (soaked in cold water)
salt and white pepper

Pea Cream

50g peas
cold water
salt

Pickled Shallots And Mushrooms

50g sugar
100ml white wine vinegar
1 packet Shimeji mushrooms
1 shallot (cut into rings)

Focaccia Toasts

1 focaccia
olive oil
sea salt

To Finish

Parmesan shavings
micro cress

6-8 dariole moulds

Method

For The Pea Mousse

Bring the cream to the boil and stir in the soaked gelatine.

Cook the peas in boiling, salted water until soft. Combine the peas and cream, then blitz. Season and pass through a fine sieve. Pour into moulds and place in the fridge to set for 2 hours.

Chef's Tip

You can change the peas for asparagus or broccoli.

For The Pickled Shallots And Mushrooms

Bring the sugar and vinegar to the boil. Remove from the heat and divide between 2 dishes containing the shallot rings and the mushrooms. Leave to cool.

For The Pea Cream

Blitz the peas, adding a small amount of water at a time, until you have a smooth paste. Season with salt and pass through a sieve.

For The Focaccia Toasts

Preheat the oven to 180°C (fan).

Thinly slice the focaccia and place on an ovenproof tray. Drizzle with olive oil and sea salt, then place in the oven until golden brown, for about 6-8 minutes.

To Serve

Carefully remove the mousse from the moulds and place in a bowl.

Garnish with the mushrooms, shallots, pea cream, toast, cress and Parmesan.

SEA REARED TROUT, MISO CARAMEL, OYSTER & PARSLEY SAUCE

SERVES 6-8

Chablis, 1er Cru, Vaillons, Domaine Vincent Dampt, 2012 (France)

Ingredients

Trout

1 filleted sea trout (skinned, pin-boned, enough for 6-8 people)
1 litre water
100g table salt
100g sugar

Oyster And Parsley Sauce

6 oysters
1 shallot (finely diced)
50ml white wine
150ml warm water
1g dashi
150ml whipping cream
40g flat leaf parsley
1½ tsp xanthan gum

Pickled Cucumber

¼ cucumber (peeled, deseeded)
100ml white wine vinegar
50g sugar

Puffed Wild Rice

20g wild rice
500ml vegetable oil

Miso Caramel

100g sugar
25ml soy sauce
25ml lime juice
100g miso paste

To Finish

French breakfast radish (shaved)
passion fruit
Sekura cress

Method

For The Trout

Bring the salt, sugar and water to the boil, then cool to room temperature. Pour over the trout, making sure all the fish is covered and leave in the liquid for 20 minutes. Rinse the trout and pat dry. Place in a vacuum pouch on full. Place in a water bath at 44°C for 10 minutes. Remove and place into iced water.

Chef's Tip

If you don't have a water bath, cling film the trout and, using a thermometer and a pan of hot water, maintain 44°C for the duration of the cooking period.

For The Oyster And Parsley Sauce

Sweat the shallot in a pan, then add the white wine and reduce. Mix the dashi with the water and add to the shallots along with the cream. Bring to the boil, then add the parsley. Remove from the heat and add the oysters. Blitz, then add the xanthan gum. Pass through a sieve into a bowl over iced water.

For The Pickled Cucumber

Bring the vinegar and sugar to the boil, then leave to cool. Dice the cucumber and place it, with the cooled liquid, into a vacuum pouch and seal. If you don't have a vac pack, leave the cucumber to pickle for a couple of hours.

For The Puffed Wild Rice

Bring the oil up to 200°C. Add the rice and remove when it has puffed, about 5 seconds.

For The Miso Caramel

Place the sugar into a pan and heat to a light caramel. Add the lime juice and soy, stir in the miso paste and pass through a fine metal sieve.

To Serve

Spread some of the miso caramel onto a plate, portion the trout and garnish with the cucumber, rice, shaved radish and cress. Finish with passion fruit and oyster sauce.

MOCHA PARFAIT, TOFFEE ICE CREAM

SERVES 6-8

Banyuls, Tradition, Tramontane NV (France)

Ingredients

Mocha Parfait

100g 70% chocolate
50ml egg yolks (2-3 eggs)
87g caster sugar
15g liquid glucose
30ml water
1 egg white
cappuccino flavouring (a few drops of)
150ml double cream (lightly whipped)

Toffee Ice Cream

500ml semi-skimmed milk
3 egg yolks
180g caster sugar
200ml double cream

Chocolate Soil

50g caster sugar
50g ground almonds
30g plain flour
25g cocoa powder
35g unsalted butter (melted)

Chocolate Ganache

110ml double cream
15g invert sugar
125g 70% chocolate
20g unsalted butter (cubed)

Biscoff Crumb

1 packet Lotus Biscoff biscuits (blitzed to a fine crumb)

Pistachio Paste

15g pistachio paste
10ml water

80ml x 25ml easy mould tubes
1 piping bag

Method

For The Mocha Parfait (Prepare ahead)

Melt the chocolate over a ***bain-marie*** or in the microwave.

Mix the egg yolks in a mixer on medium speed.

Bring 50g of the sugar, the glucose and 15ml of the water to 118°C. Gently pour the syrup over the egg yolk and whisk for 5 minutes. Fold into the chocolate.

Start whisking the egg white on medium speed.

Bring the remaining sugar and water to 121°C. Gently pour the syrup over the egg white and continue whisking for 5 minutes.

Fold the chocolate mix into the egg whites and add the cappuccino flavouring.

Finally, fold in the lightly whipped cream. Pipe into the moulds and freeze for at least 4 hours.

Chef's Tip

You can make your own tube moulds using acetate and tape.

For The Toffee Ice Cream (Prepare ahead)

Start by making the toffee sauce. Bring 50ml of cream to the boil, set aside. In a separate pan, bring 50g of sugar to a light caramel, then mix into the cream, a little at a time, ensuring you are whisking the whole time.

Mix the remaining sugar and yolks together until light and fluffy. Bring the milk to the boil and pour over the yolks, then mix in the double cream.

Pour it back into a saucepan and return to the heat, stirring continuously, until it coats the back of a wooden spoon. Add to the toffee sauce and churn in an ice cream machine. Freeze.

For The Chocolate Soil

Preheat the oven to 165°C (fan).

Mix all the ingredients together, spread out on greaseproof paper and bake for 10 minutes, mix half way through.

For The Chocolate Ganache

Bring the cream and invert sugar to the boil.

Melt the chocolate over a ***bain-marie*** or in the microwave.

Mix the cream into the chocolate until completely ***emulsified***, then mix in the butter until it has melted. Pour into a lined tray to form a thin layer and leave to set.

For The Pistachio Paste

Mix the paste and water together to form a spreadable paste.

To Serve

Using a pastry brush, spread a thin layer of pistachio paste onto a plate. Cut out a piece of ganache and place onto the paste. Remove the parfait from the mould and roll in the crumb. Place onto the ganache, spoon a little chocolate soil onto the plate and top with a scoop of toffee ice cream.

(see glossary)

MICHELIN STAR SPOTLIGHT...

DOMINIC JACK

CHEF PATRON, CASTLE TERRACE

I began my career at the prestigious Gleneagles Hotel in Perthshire as a young apprentice and spent four years learning my trade. This is where I first found my love for cooking and it inspired me to want to go to France to work and develop my skills further. I spent eight years in Paris working in some incredibly hard kitchens for chef Alain Solivérès and legendary restauranteur Monsier Jean-Claude Vrinat at the iconic 3 Michelin star Restaurant Taillvent where I held the position of sous chef. I then spent two years as head chef of the fine dining restaurant at luxurious Swissôtel in Istanbul before returning to my hometown of Edinburgh.

Back in Scotland I spent two years getting to know the very best local suppliers, preparing and planning with the vision of setting up my own restaurant. It was a proud moment when we found the right site and opened Castle Terrace Restaurant in July 2010 together with the management team behind The Kitchin. After 18 months we were awarded a Michelin star which was fantastic recognition of the entire team's hard work but also a celebration of Scottish cuisine.

From the beginning, we set out to create a level of excellence that would offer every guest a unique and memorable experience each time they visit. Our 'From Nature to Plate' philosophy allows us to focus on using the very best, local, seasonal produce as part of that commitment to excellence.

I have a huge network of great suppliers who work tirelessly to provide me with some outstanding Scottish produce. They are some of the world's most passionate and skilled producers and suppliers, and what they deliver each day really does dictate my menus - from the first grouse of the season to lobster caught just off the shores of Newhaven, a stone's throw away from our restaurant. For me, innovation and consistency are vital. The team and I are constantly looking for new ways to make the Castle Terrace experience even more memorable, striving to provide perfection in every dish we serve, with service reflecting our love for hospitality.

33/35 Castle Terrace, Edinburgh, EH1 2EL.
0131 229 1222 www.castleterracerestaurant.com

112

FONAB CASTLE HOTEL

SANDEMANS FINE DINING RESTAURANT

Foss Road, Pitlochry, Perthshire, PH16 5ND

01796 470 140
www.fonabcastlehotel.com Twitter: :@fonabcastle

Fonab Castle Hotel opened in July 2013 and soon established itself as a prominent 5 star hotel in Scotland. Nestled on the banks of Loch Faskally, Pitlochry, in the heart of Perthshire, the hotel offers 26 bedrooms including four suites and a luxurious Castle Penthouse. The hotel brasserie and lounge provide outstanding vistas of the loch itself and Sandemans 2 AA Rosette fine dining restaurant is a tranquil setting for experiencing exquisite cuisine and fine wines.

The recently launched spa at Fonab provides a haven for relaxation, pampering and rejuvenation.

With two dining options of Fonab Brasserie, a more relaxed dining area, and Sandemans Fine Dining Restaurant, head chef Paul Burns and his team have created experiences to suit all tastes. With such rich produce within the heart of Scotland's larder, Paul focuses on using quality, locally sourced ingredients with an abundance of natural flavour, creating dishes that speak for themselves. Whether it is foraging for mushrooms, picking succulent Blairgowrie berries or sourcing meat and fish locally, each ingredient Paul uses complements the other to create dishes full of intense flavours.

Nestled on the banks of Loch Faskally in the heart of Perthshire, Fonab Castle Hotel provides a tranquil setting to enjoy exquisite cuisine and fine wines.

SCOTTISH BLUE LOBSTER, POTATO & TRUFFLE SALAD

SERVES 4

Delamotte Champagne Brut (France)

Ingredients

1 x 800g Scottish Blue lobster (cooked)

Dressing

75ml virgin olive oil
75ml groundnut oil
30ml sherry vinegar
5g Dijon mustard
salt (pinch of)
sugar (pinch of)
10g honey

Potato

2 medium Red Rooster potatoes
saffron (pinch of)
salt (good pinch of)

Truffle Salad

fresh truffle (the more the better, sliced)
1 tomato (flesh diced)
1 radish (thinly sliced)
1 small red onion (thinly sliced)
herb sprigs or baby lettuce leaves
4 small wedges of lemon (optional)

Method

For The Dressing

Whisk the mustard and vinegar together. Add the honey and oils and continue to whisk. Taste and adjust the flavour with salt and sugar.

For The Potatoes

Peel the potatoes, wash them and cut into small discs, allowing 2 per person. Place in a pan with the saffron, salt and cold water and bring to the boil. Simmer until cooked. When cooked, remove carefully from the water and place in the dressing. This must be done when potatoes are hot to take on the flavours. Allow potatoes to cool.

For The Lobster

Carefully remove the meat from the shell and divide into 4 portions.

Chef's Tip

If lobster is not available, you may substitute with prawns.

To Serve

Place the potato discs on plates, taking care not to add too much dressing and place the lobster on top.

Arrange the tomato, radish, onion, leaves and lemon (if using) on the plate. Add the sliced truffle to finish. Serve and enjoy.

PRIME BEEF FILLET, FOIE GRAS, ROASTED VEGETABLES & MORELS

SERVES 4

Bodegas Belezos Rioja Crianza 2011 (Spain)

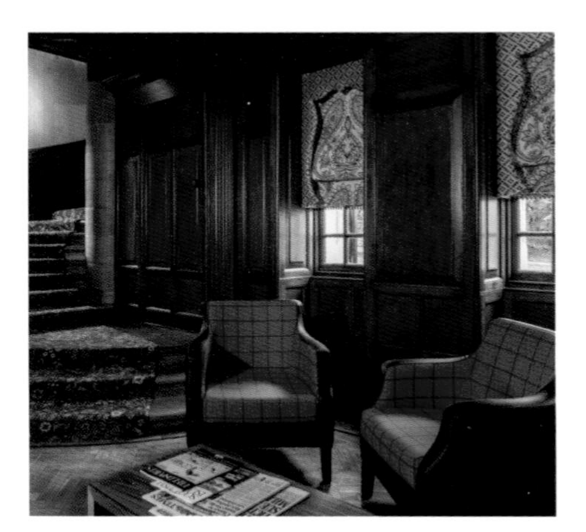

Ingredients

Beef And Foie Gras

4 x 150g fillet steaks
4 x 40g foie gras (optional)
salt and pepper
vegetable oil

Madeira And Red Wine Sauce

4 shallots (thinly sliced)
butter (knob of)
50ml Madeira
200ml good red wine
1 sprig thyme
300ml good beef stock

Vegetables

your choice of vegetables (*blanched*, cooked *al dente*)
morel mushrooms (gently brushed to remove any dust)
butter (to coat)

Method

To Prepare The Beef Fillet

Take the beef out of the fridge 30 minutes prior to cooking to bring up to room temperature. Season the steaks on both sides with salt and pepper.

For The Madeira And Red Wine Sauce

Gently fry the shallots in butter until tender. Stir in the Madeira and reduce to a syrup. Add the wine, then reduce further. Pour in half the stock along with the thyme and continue to reduce to a syrup consistency. Pass through a fine sieve and taste.

The sauce should be rich in flavour. If more flavour is required, add more stock and reduce further.

To Serve

Heat a frying pan until hot, add a little oil and fry the steak on both sides to your required taste. Leave to rest and keep warm.

Heat another frying pan, season the foie gras and fry until golden brown. Place the beef and foie gras onto a plate, then fry the mushrooms in the foie gras pan.

Reheat the vegetables in butter and arrange on the plate alongside the fried mushrooms. Finally, drizzle the sauce over the plate.

Chef's Tip

If morels are not available, use your favourite mushrooms.

(see glossary)

LEMON & ORANGE POSSET, LEMON SORBET, TUILE TWISTS & BERRIES

SERVES 4

 *Chateau Septy Monbazillac 2010 (France)*

Ingredients

Lemon And Orange Posset

500ml double cream
125g caster sugar
2 lemons (juice and zest of)
1 orange (zest of)

Tuile Twist Biscuits

50g caster sugar
50g plain flour
50g butter
50g egg whites (from 1-2 eggs)

Lemon Sorbet

175ml water
175g caster sugar
30g glucose
2 lemons (juice and zest of)

Garnish

seasonal berries
red vein sorrel

4 glasses

Method

For The Lemon And Orange Posset

Warm cream with the sugar, lemon juice and zest and gently simmer for 2 minutes. Pass through a fine sieve and leave to cool. When cool, divide into 4 glasses and place in the fridge to set for 2 hours.

Chef's Tip

Always wash your citrus fruit before using.

For The Tuile Twist Biscuits

Preheat the oven to 180°C.

Place all ingredients into a food processor and blend until smooth. Place the mixture into the fridge until it firms and feels thick in consistency. Using a palate knife, thinly scrape the mixture onto a baking mat in 'finger-like' strips.

Bake for 2-3 minutes then remove from the oven and carefully twist the tuile around a wooden spoon handle to make the twists in the biscuits. This will need to be done quickly, when still warm, to ensure the biscuit is pliable around the handle. Leave to cool.

For The Lemon Sorbet

Bring the water, sugar and glucose slowly to the boil, simmer for 5 minutes, then leave to cool. Once cool, add the lemon juice and churn in an ice cream machine.

To Serve

Scoop some sorbet into each glass of posset. Decorate with a few berries, tuile twist biscuit and sorrel and enjoy!

122
LA GARRIGUE

31 Jeffrey Street, Edinburgh, EH1 1DH

0131 557 3032
www.lagarrigue.co.uk Twitter: @lagarriguerest

La Garrigue opened in 2001 under the ownership of chef J-Michel Gauffre, a member of the Academy of Culinary arts. This small, welcoming neighbourhood bistro/restaurant has since won many pundits and has become an institution. J-Michel's provincial, rustic style cooking is complemented by Tim Stead's wooden furniture and Andrew Walker's paintings from villages in Languedoc. The ever changing menus offer a selection of dishes inspired from J-Michel's culinary heritage of Languedoc and offer specialities such as fish soup, Roquefort soufflés, rabbit, bouillabaisse, cassoulet, poutargue and lavender desserts. This fusion cooking of southern France and Scottish produce has won J-Michel and his team many awards over the years but the highlight was the inclusion of La Garrigue in Gordon Ramsay's Best Restaurant television series.

The award-winning wine list has been designed to match the style and origin of the food and is entirely compiled from handpicked selection of Languedoc best vineyards and appellations, carefully chosen by J-Michel during his frequents visits and wine tours in Languedoc. Arguably the most authentic French restaurant in town,
La Garrigue is situated a few yards from the famous Royal Mile and boasts amazing views of Calton Hill and the Edinburgh skyline.

31

LA garrigue

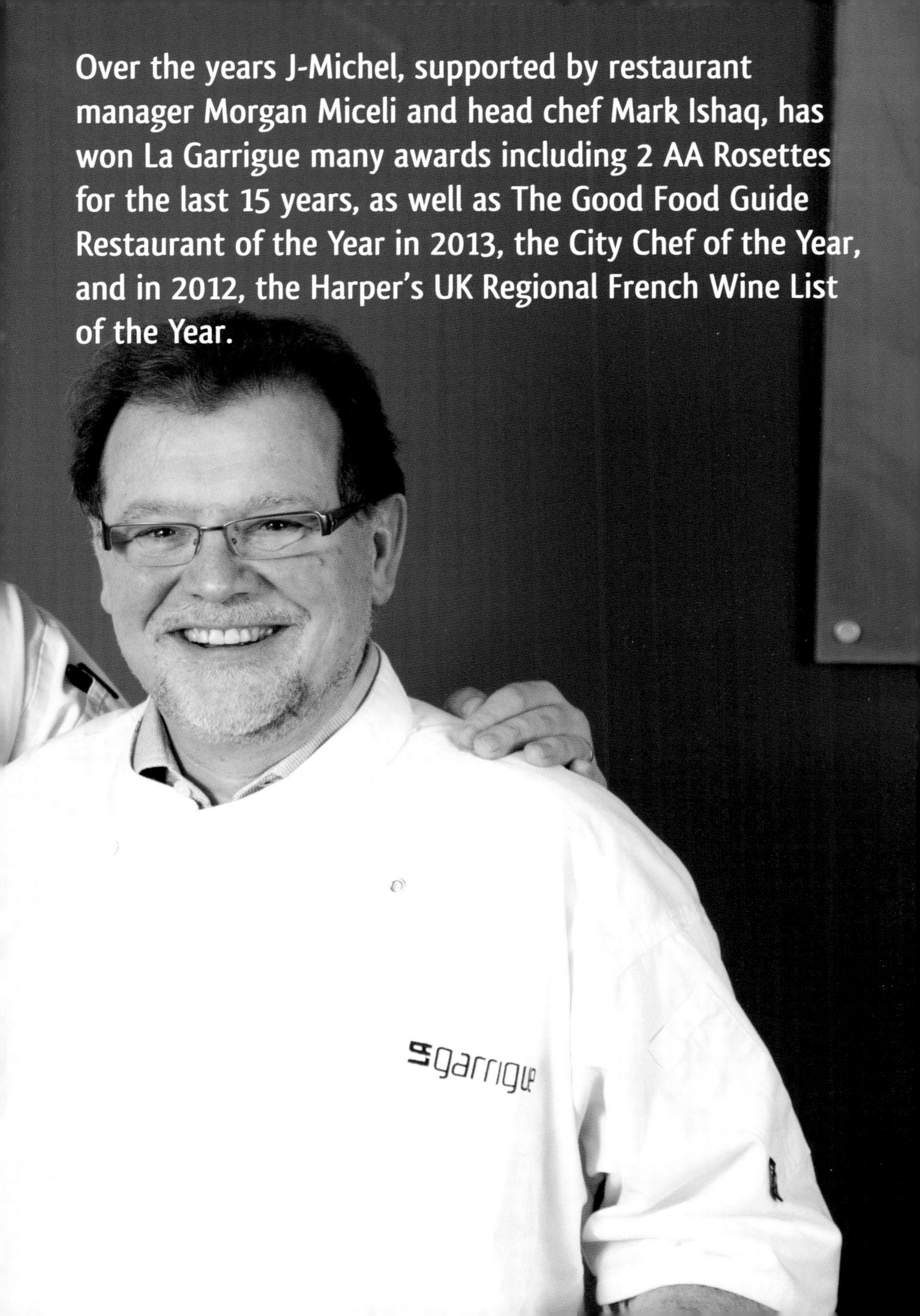

Over the years J-Michel, supported by restaurant manager Morgan Miceli and head chef Mark Ishaq, has won La Garrigue many awards including 2 AA Rosettes for the last 15 years, as well as The Good Food Guide Restaurant of the Year in 2013, the City Chef of the Year, and in 2012, the Harper's UK Regional French Wine List of the Year.

HAND DIVED SCALLOPS WITH BLACK PUDDING & CHICORY, VERMOUTH & ORANGE BUTTER

SERVES 4

 *Les Aires, Viognier 2012, Domaine de Clovallon (France)*

Ingredients

12 hand dived scallops (white meat only)
50g unsalted butter
1 orange (juice of)
40ml Noilly Prat Vermouth
150g French or Stornoway black pudding (cut into small dice)
4 medium red chicory (sliced)
chervil (bunch of)

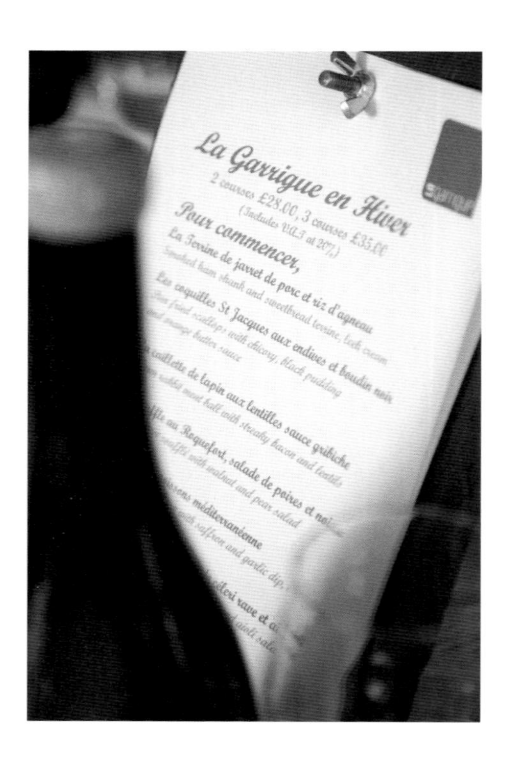

Method

For The Scallops

Season the scallops and pan fry them in a non-stick pan with the butter for a couple of minutes on each side to give them a nice caramel colour. Remove from the pan and reserve. In the same pan, warm the black pudding, then add the sliced chicory and cook for a few seconds to give a wilted effect.

Remove and keep with the scallops.

Add the orange juice and Vermouth to the pan and reduce.

To Serve

Place the black pudding and chicory on a plate. Place 3 scallops on top and pour over the reduced sauce. Decorate with the chervil and enjoy with a glass of chilled Viognier.

Chef's Tip

Use the freshest scallops from your local fishmonger. Remove the roe and keep to make a bisque or fish stew.

SLOW COOKED LAMB SHANK WITH CHICKPEAS, CARROTS & TARRAGON

SERVES 4

Felines, La Borie de Maurel, 2011 (France)

Ingredients

Lamb

4 lamb shanks
butter (to coat)
olive oil (to coat)
3 onions (roughly diced)
3 carrots (roughly diced)
3 cloves garlic
2 bay leaves
3 sprigs thyme
1 litre red wine
1½ litres water
500g pig caul
300g mushrooms (finely chopped)
2 tbsp Dijon mustard
olive oil (to fry)

Chickpeas, Carrots And Tarragon

500g dried chickpeas (soaked overnight)
3 cloves garlic
3 bay leaves
4 carrots
142ml double cream
fresh tarragon (bunch of)

4 consommé cups or bavarois moulds

Method

For The Chickpeas, Carrots And Tarragon (Prepare ahead)

Rinse the soaked chickpeas and place in a stockpot. Cover with water and add the garlic and bay leaves. Cook, skimming the water of any impurities, until tender and soft. Cut the carrots into small dice, the size of the chickpeas, and cook them in boiling water until tender. Reserve them with the cooked chickpeas.

Chef's Tip

Soak the chickpeas overnight and wash well in running water before cooking.

For The Lamb (Prepare ahead)

Preheat the oven to 135°C.

Place the lamb shanks in a roasting tray. Coat them with some butter and olive oil. Add 2 of the onions, the carrots, garlic and herbs and roast in the oven for 3-4 hours until the meat falls off the bone, taking care while turning and basting them during the cooking process. When cooked, remove from the roasting tray and leave to cool. Remove the meat from the bone and reserve on a plate. Put the bones back into the tray, then add the wine and the water and bring to the boil. Strain into a clean pan and reduce until the stock is thick.

Wash the pig caul and line 4 consommé cups or bavarois moulds.

Cook the remaining diced onion in a little olive oil in a pan with the mushrooms. When cooked, add into the shredded lamb meat, along with the mustard. Season and press the meat into the lined moulds. Allow to cool, then refrigerate until required.

To Serve

Preheat the oven to 180°C.

Heat up the cream, add the tarragon, then the chickpeas and carrots. Keep hot.

Remove the meat from the moulds, place on a baking tray in the oven and heat for 5-8 minutes until hot.

Using a metal ring, arrange the chickpeas and carrots on a serving plate. Place the meat on top, pour over the sauce and serve with a glass of Felines, La Borie de Maurel.

LAVENDER CREME BRULEE

SERVES 4

Blanquette de Limoux (France)

Ingredients

Lavender Crème Brûlée

500ml whipping cream
½ tsp lavender flowers
4 egg yolks
25g sugar

To Serve

caramel powder or caster sugar
tuile or shortbread biscuits
seasonal berries

4 ramekins

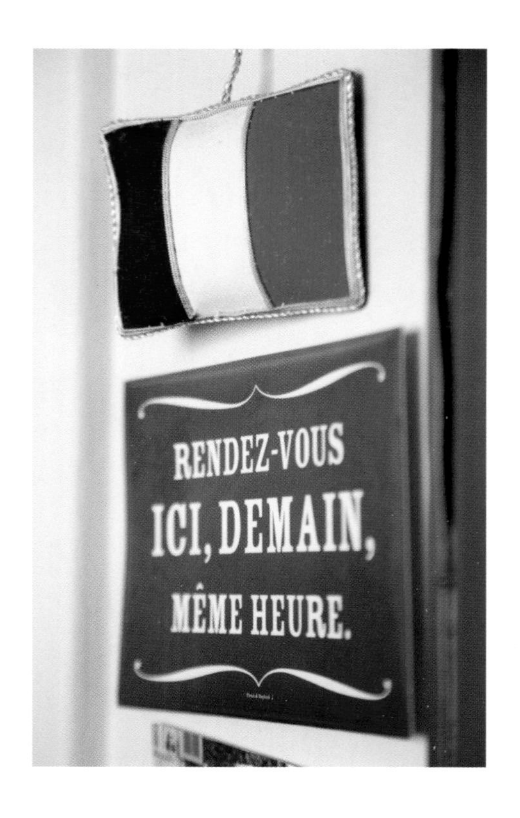

Method

For The Lavender Crème Brûlée

Preheat the oven to 140°C.

Bring the cream and lavender flowers to the boil.

Mix the egg yolks and the sugar, beating well until light and fluffy.

Slowly pour the cream onto the egg mixture. Carefully heat on a low heat until the mixture coats the back of a wooden spoon, then pour into the ramekins. Place the ramekins into a deep oven tray and fill the tray with water to half way up the ramekin dishes. Bake in the oven for 20 minutes or until set. Leave to cool.

To Serve

Sprinkle with the sugar or caramel powder and glaze with a blow torch. Serve with shortbread or tuile biscuits and berries.

MICHELIN STAR SPOTLIGHT...

TOM KITCHIN

CHEF OWNER, THE KITCHIN

I spent many years learning from some of the greatest French masters, including the legendary Michelin star chefs Pierre Koffmann and Alain Ducasse in London, France and Monaco. However, the highlight of my career was definitely the day my wife Michaela and I opened The Kitchin restaurant in Leith in my hometown of Edinburgh. From day one, we've lived and breathed our 'From Nature to Plate' philosophy and we're truly committed to only using the very best of Scotland's produce taken straight from our land and seas.

Nine years since opening, we've just refurbished and expanded The Kitchin which has been a really exciting step for us. Although the restaurant has grown, our commitment to excellence is still at the core. Not only has the dining room and bar had a complete makeover but we've also introduced a private dining room, whisky snug and wine cellar. It has allowed us to enhance the experience for the guests, and given us the chance to ensure the restaurant decor and front of house also reflect our 'From Nature to Plate' food philosophy which we feel so passionate about. The expanded kitchen now holds state of the art equipment and a butchery area, which allows us to do all the butchering in-house and continuously evolve our menus. Over the years, The Kitchin has received numerous awards including a Michelin star and 4 AA Rosettes, 'Best UK Restaurant' and most recently 'Best Restaurant Experience 2015'.

We're truly fanatical about seasonality and I firmly believe that Scotland's natural larder is, without doubt, one of the best in the world. In the past decade, Scotland's reputation for producing the finest quality food and drink has grown significantly, putting Scottish restaurants, chefs and suppliers on the world's culinary map. We're as passionate as ever about flying the flag for Scotland, promoting its outstanding seasonal produce.

78 Commercial Quay, Leith, Edinburgh, EH6 6LX.
0131 555 1755 www.thekitchin.com

134 GLENAPP CASTLE

Ballantrae, Ayrshire, KA26 0NZ

01465 831 212
www.glenappcastle.com Twitter: @GlenappCastle Facebook: Glenapp Castle

Glenapp Castle, renowned for 15 years as one of Scotland's finest country house hotels, is a truly majestic, towered and be-turreted castle in the finest Hogwartian tradition. Its mellow sandstone battlements and spectacular views across the Irish Sea have earned Glenapp its rightful place as one of the most romantic castles in Scotland. Luxurious bedrooms and suites and achingly beautiful gardens combine with one of the country's finest dining rooms to create a magical experience for guests who travel to this unspoiled corner of south west Scotland. Head chef Tyron Ellul came to Glenapp two years ago and his modern British style, using classic marriages of flavours with inventive twists, results in spectacular dishes and a well-deserved reputation for fine dining.

Tyron and his team, in their first year together, earned 3 AA Rosettes and more importantly, a loyal following of regular guests. Every day, the small team of chefs prepare superb lunches and afternoon teas for resident guests and day visitors alike, and in the evenings serve three or six course gourmet dinner menus that showcase the best fresh and seasonal local ingredients. Tyron makes excellent use of the spectacular local produce available, such as lobster and crab from Ballantrae Bay, beef and lamb from local farms, wonderful cheeses, some from very nearby and all of the others from around Scotland, and fruit, vegetables and herbs from the castle's one hectare walled garden and glasshouses.

Imagine... a fairytale castle, outstanding cuisine, fine wines and exceptional service - Glenapp Castle - a world apart.

PAN SEARED FILLET OF SEA BASS WITH SAFFRON CONSOMME & BUTTER POACHED BALLANTRAE LOBSTER

SERVES 4

Albariño, Castel de Bouza, Galicia (Spain)

Ingredients

Lobster

4 Ballantrae lobster claws
water and butter *emulsion*

Sea Bass

2 large sea bass fillets
vegetable oil
foaming butter

Saffron Consommé

2 onions (chopped)
2 sticks celery (chopped)
½ fennel bulb (sliced)
2 bay leaves
6 peppercorns
olive oil (drizzle of)
1kg white fish bones
1 litre water
4 egg whites
300g white fish flesh
12 saffron strands
salt (pinch of)

Pasta And Vegetables

150g hand cut squid ink linguini
20 carrots (shaped with Parisiènne cutter)
20 tips samphire
6 tips wild asparagus

Garnish

chives (chopped)
chive blossom
olive oil (drizzle of)

Method

For The Saffron Consommé

Sweat the vegetables in a little olive oil without colouring them. Add in the water, bay leaves, peppercorns and fish bones and simmer for around 20 minutes. Pass the stock through a sieve and keep to the side.

Blitz the fish flesh with the egg whites in a food processor. Bring the stock to a gentle simmer, then whisk in the fish and egg white mixture. Allow to cook until a cake forms and floats on the surface. Gently pass this clarified stock through muslin. Season with salt and saffron.

For The Pasta And Vegetables

Blanch the squid ink linguini and the vegetables in separate pans.

To Serve

Sear the sea bass fillets, skin-side down, and pan fry in a little vegetable oil and foaming butter. Warm the lobster claws in a water and butter *emulsion* along with the *blanched* squid ink linguini, then gently warm up the *blanched* vegetables. Roll the linguini on a fork and place in the centre of a bowl. Neatly arrange the seared fillet of sea bass and lobster claw on top of the linguine.

Arrange the vegetables around the bowl, then gently pour over the saffron consommé. Sprinkle with chopped chives and chive blossom and drizzle with a little olive oil.

Chef's Tip

For a crystal clear consommé, use a *chinois* to break into the raft, then gently ladle the stock through another *chinois* lined with muslin cloth. Look for good quality, fresh fish from a trusted fishmonger. You can ask him to fillet the sea bass for you, but make sure you keep the bones.

(see glossary)

RED WINE BRAISED FEATHER BLADE OF BEEF WITH SAUTEED MUSHROOMS, GNOCCHI & RED WINE REDUCTION

SERVES 4

Château Garraud, Lalande de Pomerol, Bordeaux, 2006 (France)

Ingredients

Braised Beef

1kg feather blade beef
2 onions (chopped)
3 cloves garlic (chopped)
2 celery sticks (chopped)
2 carrots (chopped)
1 leek (chopped)
2 bay leaves
1 bunch thyme
4 peppercorns
1 litre red wine
500ml port
1 litre chicken stock
250g *crepinette*

Gnocchi

100g mashed potatoes
50g 00 flour
10g thyme leaf (chopped)
40g Parmesan (grated)
2 egg yolks
flour (to dust)

Onion Purée

500g white onions (peeled, finely sliced)
100g butter
100ml cream

To Serve

100g white onion purée
4 spring onions (griddled)
100g mushrooms (sautéed)
carrots (roasted)

Method

For The Braised Beef (Prepare 2 days ahead)

Trim excess sinew from the feather blade of beef and colour in a hot frying pan. Set aside. Sweat off the ***mirepoix*** of vegetables, add the bay leaves, thyme, peppercorns, wine and port and reduce by half. Once cooled, add the beef and let it marinate overnight.

Add the chicken stock to the marinade and braise the beef in a low oven at 140°C (fan) for 4 hours. Allow to cool in the cooking liquor, then remove the excess gristle from the centre. Roll the blade in cling film and allow to rest overnight in the fridge.

Reduce the cooking liquor to a sticky sauce. Slice the beef and remove the cling film, then roll the beef medallions in the *crepinette*. Colour the *crepinette* covered medallions in a pan, then warm them in the cooking reduction. Reserve the cooking liquor to serve.

Chef's Tip

Make sure the beef blade is wrapped up nice and tight in cling film and is well chilled, preferably overnight. As beef blade is not a very common cut, you might need to order it in advance with your trusted local butcher.

For The Gnocchi

Combine the potatoes and 00 flour, stir in the chopped thyme and Parmesan. Add in the egg yolks to form a dough. Weigh the mixture into 10g dumplings then, on a lightly floured surface, shape with the aid of a fork. ***Blanch*** the gnocchi in a pan of boiling, salted water for 2 minutes or until they float to the surface.

For The Onion Purée

Gently sweat the onions in butter until they turn translucent. When the onions are cooked, add in the cream and cook until the cream reduces by half. Blitz in a food processor, correct the seasoning and pass through a fine sieve.

To Serve

Swipe a portion of onion purée along the centre of a warmed plate. Place a griddled spring onion on the onion purée, then gently lay the warmed beef blade on top. Neatly arrange the gnocchi and the sautéed mushrooms around the beef and finish the dish with carrots and the reduced cooking liquor.

(see glossary)

SPICED PINEAPPLE CARPACCIO WITH MUSCOVADO SPONGE CAKE & COCONUT ICE CREAM

SERVES 4

 *Coteaux Du Layon, Carte d'Or, Domaine des Baumard (France)*

Ingredients

Coconut Ice Cream

4 egg yolks
200g caster sugar
500ml double cream
250ml coconut milk

Pineapple Carpaccio

300g muscovado sugar
50g honey
1 litre water
½ red chilli
2 star anise
1 vanilla pod
1 pineapple (peeled)
50ml dark rum

Muscovado Sponge Cake

200g muscovado sugar
200g butter
200g self-raising flour
salt (pinch of)
4 eggs

Garnish

coriander cress

30cm x 30cm cake tin (lined)

Method

For The Coconut Ice Cream (Prepare 1 day ahead)

Whisk the egg yolks and sugar together. Warm the cream and coconut milk, then pour onto the egg yolks. Transfer back to a gentle heat and cook until it reaches 82°C. Remove from the heat and cool. Strain and allow to mature overnight before churning in an ice cream machine.

For The Pineapple Carpaccio

Preheat the oven to 160°C (fan).

Combine the sugar and honey and cook to a light caramel. Add in the water, spices and vanilla pod and simmer over a low heat. Place the peeled pineapple into a deep, ovenproof tray. Pour the spiced syrup and rum on top. Cover with tin foil and bake for approximately 1 hour, basting the pineapple at 20 minute intervals. Once the pineapple is cooked it should feel soft to the touch. Allow to cool in the cooking liquor.

For The Muscovado Sponge Cake

Preheat the oven to 180°C (fan).

Beat the sugar and butter together until pale and fluffy. Add in the flour and salt, then gradually add in the eggs one at a time. Pour the mixture into the prepared tin and bake for 15-20 minutes.

To Serve

Thinly slice the pineapple and arrange 4 slices in the centre of a large plate.

Cut the sponge cake into rectangles and warm in a microwave for a few seconds. Place on top of the pineapple carpaccio. Lastly, scoop a serving of coconut ice cream, drizzle the plate with some of the pineapple cooking liquor and garnish with the coriander cress.

Chef's Tip

Make sure you use a ripe pineapple for the dish so you get the benefit of the natural sweetness from the fruit. Use good quality muscovado sugar for the cake and it will give the sponge a lovely, deep molasses flavour.

144 HAMILTON'S BAR & KITCHEN

16-18 Hamilton Place, Stockbridge, Edinburgh, EH3 5AU

0131 226 4199
www.hamiltonsedinburgh.co.uk
Twitter: @HamiltonsEdin Facebook: Hamilton's Bar and Kitchen Instagram: Hamiltons Edinburgh

When Colin Church and Martin Luney opened Hamilton's in 2008, they set upon Stockbridge as their ideal location. Taking its name from the old Scots word for 'wooden footbridge' after the original bridge that crossed over from the water of Leith, work on the Stockbridge we see today began in 1801.

Despite being 10 minutes from the city centre, there is a definite village vibe to Stockbridge. Over the years many noted artists, poets and musicians have made the area their home, including Sir Henry Raeburn, Chopin and poet James Hogg, to name a few. Due to its picturesque setting, the village has been used as a location for many films and television series, including the Oscar winning 'The Prime of Miss Jean Brodie' and the much loved 'Rebus'.

As an independent bar and kitchen, Hamilton's is perfectly suited to the area. With the famous Stockbridge clock, adorned on the customised Roy Lichtenstein inspired mural, Hamilton's carries itself with an individual style, a relaxed atmosphere and great food and drinks.

The bar prides itself on a seasonal approach to menu design. Food and cocktail menus change with the seasons and take advantage of local techniques and suppliers, whilst remaining innovative with a home prepared feel.

The company, Big Red Teapot Ltd, has become one of the city's great success stories of recent years. Encompassing Hamilton's Bar and Kitchen, Treacle and The Blackbird - the group has become one of the kingpins of the city's new independent eating and drinking set, winning Scottish Style Awards, Young Entrepreneur of the Year, Best Group Bar Employer and many cocktail competitions and showcases.

SAFFRON & SCOTTISH ALE BATTERED WEST COAST OYSTERS, RED CHILLI JAM

SERVES 4

Innis & Gunn Oak Aged Beer.
Grassy hops, vanilla and mild fruit to balance the mild spices and complement the freshness of the oysters.

Ingredients

Oysters

20 oysters
flour (to coat)

Red Chilli Jam

6 red chillies (seeds removed, sliced)
1 clove garlic (crushed)
1 ball stem ginger (sliced)
1 tbsp olive oil
1 tbsp tomato purée
400g caster sugar
50ml distilled vinegar
300ml water

Saffron And Scottish Ale Batter

1 bottle Scottish Ale (we used Innis & Gunn Original)
300ml soda water
50ml white wine vinegar
½g saffron
180g plain flour
salt and black pepper (pinch of)

To Serve

50g kale (steamed)

Method

For The Red Chilli Jam

Heat the oil in a non-stick pan. Add the chillies, garlic, ginger and tomato purée and gently heat for 3-4 minutes. Add the vinegar, sugar and water. Leave to cook on a medium heat for 20 minutes, stirring occasionally, until it reaches a jam consistency. Remove from the heat. Blend until smooth and leave to cool before storing in an air tight container.

For The Saffron And Scottish Ale Batter

Pour the ale, soda and saffron in to a round bottomed bowl. Leave to stand for a few minutes. Next, add the white wine vinegar and slowly add the flour - whisking continuously until thick. Season with a pinch of salt and pepper.

Chef's Tip

To ensure a crispy batter, add a splash of acid, such as vinegar or fresh lemon juice.

For The Oysters

Hold the oyster in a cloth, rounded side down, and insert a knife (always use an oyster knife) between the 2 shells near the hinge. Twist the knife to separate the shells. Sever the muscle that connects the oyster to the shell, then slide the knife blade underneath the oyster to detach it.

Keep the oysters and the juice to one side. Wash the rounded shell and dry out thoroughly.

Pat the oysters dry, then lightly coat in flour and dip in the batter. Carefully place in a deep fat fryer set at 180ºC. Cook for no longer than 40-50 seconds. Remove the oysters and pat dry on paper. Season to taste. (Be careful as the oysters are naturally salty).

To Serve

Serve the oysters as pictured with the steamed kale and chilli jam.

PERTHSHIRE VENISON HAUNCH WITH HAGGIS & OATMEAL FRITTERS, SMASHED BUTTERNUT SQUASH, RED BERRY JUS & PARSNIP CRISPS

SERVES 4

Terre da Vino, Barolo, 2010 (Italy)
Italian reds work well here - we're fans of Barolo. Savoury and full bodied with hints of truffle and smoke.

Ingredients

Venison

680g venison haunch
1 clove garlic (sliced)
1 sprig fresh rosemary (chopped)
30ml olive oil
salt and pepper

Butternut Squash

1 butternut squash

Haggis Fritters

150g haggis
2-3 tbsp plain flour (to coat)
2 free range eggs (lightly beaten)
50g pinhead oatmeal (to coat)
salt and pepper

Red Berry Jus

200ml veal jus
50ml red wine
1 tbsp redcurrant jelly
25g fresh redcurrants

Parsnip Crisps

1 large parsnip

Method

To Prepare The Venison (Prepare in advance)

Combine the garlic with the rosemary and the olive oil. Rub on to the venison and leave to marinate overnight, or for a minimum of 3-4 hours.

For The Butternut Squash

Preheat the oven to 190°C.

Cut the squash lengthways with a firm grip of the knife and remove the seeds with a dessertspoon. Season and wrap both halves in tin foil. Place in the oven for 20-30 minutes, or until soft to touch. Scoop out the squash using a spoon and keep warm.

For The Haggis

Roll the haggis into bite size balls using the palms of your hands. Lightly coat in flour, then dip in the beaten egg, followed by the oatmeal. This can be repeated if not totally coated. Deep fry at 180°C until golden. Pat dry to remove any excess oil and season to taste.

For The Parsnip Crisps

Peel the outer skin from the parsnip and discard. Continue to peel along the full length of the parsnip to get long, even ribbons. Gently fry at 160°C until there is no movement in the fryer. Drain onto kitchen paper and season.

For The Venison And Red Berry Jus

Preheat the oven to 190°C.

Rub any excess marinade off the venison. Sear in a hot pan on both sides for 2-3 minutes. Transfer to a tray and keep warm in the oven for a further 3-4 minutes. Remove from the oven and allow the meat to relax for 3-4 minutes.

Pour the red wine into the still hot pan and reduce by half. Whisk in the redcurrant jelly and veal jus. Leave on the heat for 2-3 minutes before adding fresh redcurrants.

To Serve

Serve as pictured.

Chef's Tip

Feel free to use different berries in your jus as the seasons progress to ring the changes throughout the year.

LEMON & TOASTED ALMOND MOUSSE WITH BUTTER & THYME SHORTBREAD

SERVES 6

'Plum Bramble' (NB Gin (North Berwick), fresh lemon, sugar and plum liqueur). The drink's flavours complement the almonds and thyme perfectly here.

Ingredients

Lemon And Toasted Almond Mousse

2 unwaxed lemons (zest and juice of)
4 medium organic eggs (separated)
215g caster sugar
10g leaf gelatine (soaked in cold water)
275ml double cream

Butter And Thyme Shortbread

225g unsalted butter
110g caster sugar
110g cornflour
225g plain flour
10g thyme (picked)
salt (pinch of)

Garnish

50g flaked almonds (toasted)

6 ramekin dishes or teacups
greaseproof paper
2 baking trays

Method

For The Lemon And Toasted Almond Mousse

Prepare a ramekin or teacup by tying a wide strip of oiled greaseproof paper around the outside top edge with string so that it extends about 2½ cm above the top of the dish or cup.

Finely grate the zest of the lemons and squeeze the juice into a bowl. Add the zest, egg yolks and sugar to the lemon juice and whisk over a *bain-marie* until the mixture thickens and turns a very light colour. Dissolve the gelatine in a few drops of boiling water, then stir into the lemon mixture and remove from the heat.

Lightly whisk the double cream until it forms soft peaks. Separately beat the egg whites until stiff. Stir the lemon mixture frequently until it is almost set. Gently fold in the cream and egg whites.

Pour the mixture into the prepared dishes so that it comes above the level of the ramekin or cup. Leave to chill in the fridge for a minimum of 2 hours.

For The Butter And Thyme Shortbread

Lightly butter 2 baking trays, or line with baking parchment.

Mix the butter and sugar together in a large bowl until light and fluffy. Sieve the flour and cornflour into the bowl, then add the salt and thyme. Mix together until well combined and smooth. Tip the mixture out onto a lightly floured surface and knead to a soft dough.

Roll out the dough between 2 pieces of baking parchment to a thickness of 1cm. Prick the dough all over with a fork and cut into biscuit shapes. Roll the remaining dough to cut more. Place the shortbreads on the prepared baking trays and chill for 30 minutes.

Preheat the oven to 170°C.

Bake the shortbreads for 20 minutes until just turning golden brown. Leave on the baking trays for a few minutes, then place the shortbreads onto a wire rack. Dust with sugar and leave to cool.

Chef's Tip

When making shortbread, make sure your butter is cold. This will allow for a shorter and more crumbly biscuit.

To Serve

Carefully remove the paper collars from the ramekins or cups and decorate the sides with toasted almonds.

(see glossary)

154
THE KITCHIN

78 Commercial Quay, Leith, Edinburgh EH6 6LX.

0131 555 1755
www.thekitchin.com Twitter: @TomKitchin

ichelin star restaurant The Kitchin was opened in 2006 on Edinburgh's Leith waterfront by husband and wife Tom and Michaela Kitchin. Both with years of experience in the hospitality industry and genuinely fanatical about quality, seasonal food and providing the very highest levels of service, they have truly put Scotland on the British culinary map.

Over the last nine years, the team has been on an incredible journey, establishing the restaurant as one of the best in the country. Born from customer demand, they unveiled an extensive expansion and refurbishment of The Kitchin in January 2015, which allows for chef Tom Kitchin to continue serving guests his award-winning cuisine. The beautifully designed restaurant, which showcases fabrics, wallpapers and sheepskins from Scotland in a stylish Scottish Scandi fashion, has created the ultimate dining experience for each and every guest.

CASTLE TERRACE

In July 2010, chef patron Dominic Jack and the team behind The Kitchin, opened sister restaurant Castle Terrace in the centre of Edinburgh. Offering Scottish French cuisine, the menu reflects Michelin star chef Dominic Jack's many years of training in some of the world's best kitchens, and showcases his commitment to perfection on the plate.

The Kitchin, Castle Terrace and The Scran & Scallie Photography: Marc Millar

With their shared philosophy 'From Nature to Plate', both restaurants present menus that are always seasonal and rely on the best suppliers in Scotland to provide the highest quality, freshest, and most flavoursome produce there is. The passionate chefs pride themselves on the produce arriving at the restaurants daily, straight from the land or shores of Scotland.

THE SCRAN & SCALLIE

In March 2013, The Kitchin and Castle Terrace Restaurant teams opened gastro-pub The Scran & Scallie. The award-winning pub, which is located in Edinburgh's Stockbridge, presents a warm, family-friendly atmosphere with interiors to match. Menus are developed by Tom Kitchin and Dominic Jack, together with head chef James Chapman, and include traditional homemade Scottish scran (food). The gastro-pub has proved an absolute hit with locals and visitors from all over the country.

CASTLE TERRACE RESTAURANT

33-35 Castle Terrace, Edinburgh, EH1 2EL.
0131 229 1222 www.castleterracerestaurant.com
Twitter: @dominicjack

Castle Terrace Restaurant opened its doors in July 2010 introducing a new dining experience to the city of Edinburgh. Nestled underneath Edinburgh Castle, the restaurant, led by chef patron Dominic Jack, was awarded a Michelin star in October 2011. Castle Terrace offers a menu based on Chef Jack's innovative creations influenced by French cooking techniques and Scotland's natural larder.

WILD SCOTTISH SALMON TARTARE SERVED SUSHI STYLE

Dominic Jack, Castle Terrace Restaurant
33-35 Castle Terrace, Edinburgh, EH1 2EL.
0131 229 1222 www.castleterracerestaurant.com Twitter: @dominicjack

SERVES 4

Vacqueyras Blanc 'Mineral', Domaine Montirius, Rhone Valley, 2012 (France)

Ingredients

240g fresh Scottish salmon (finely diced, seasoned)

Crispy Rice
200g rice, plain flour (to dust)
oil (to deep fry), salt (to season)

Wasabi Ice Cream
375ml milk, 375ml double cream
140g egg yolks (from about 7 eggs)
30g wasabi, 10g sugar
2 large handfuls spinach, salt (pinch of)

Soy Jelly
300ml soy sauce, 200ml water
12g agar agar or 5 sheets gelatine (soaked until soft, excess water squeezed out)

Sesame Oil Dressing
120g honey, 80ml sherry vinegar
150ml sesame seed oil, 150ml olive oil

Pickled Carrots
100ml white wine vinegar, 1 litre water
20g salt, 250g sugar
2 bay leaves, 10 black peppercorns
100g carrots (peeled, julienne)

Lime Crisps
50ml simple stock syrup, 1 lime (frozen)

Pickled Ginger
40 ginger batons (cut into little dice)
30ml simple stock syrup

Garnish
4 tsp black sesame seeds
4 coriander leaves (deep fried until crispy)
1 whole cucumber

Method

For The Crispy Rice
Cook the rice in salted water until soft, plunge in cold water and drain. Spread the cold rice out on kitchen paper and dry thoroughly. Lightly coat in flour. Deep fry in oil (80°C) until crispy. Season with salt.

For The Wasabi Ice Cream (Prepare ahead)
Bring the milk and cream slowly to the boil. Whisk in the yolks, then add the other ingredients. Whilst continually whisking, bring to 86°C. Cool over ice, transfer to a suitable container and freeze for 24 hours.

For The Soy Jelly
Heat the soy sauce and water in a pan. Stir in the gelatine, pass through a sieve and set in a shallow container for 2 hours. Once set, cut into small cubes.

For The Sesame Oil Dressing
Blend the honey and vinegar together, slowly adding the oils until combined. Season with salt.

For The Pickled Carrots
Combine all the ingredients, apart from the carrots, in a heavy bottomed pan and bring to the boil. Simmer for 20 minutes, taste and add more vinegar if desired. Pour the boiling liquid over the carrots, cover with cling film and leave to cool.

For The Lime Crisps (Prepare ahead)
Finely slice the frozen lime, brush with stock syrup and cook in the oven (80°C) overnight. Cool on a mat.

For The Pickled Ginger
Bring a pan of cold water to the boil and *blanch* the ginger in water 10 times. Cover the ginger in stock syrup.

For The Cucumber Balls
Carve mini balls from the cucumber, *blanch* in boiling water, then brush with sesame oil dressing.

To Assemble The Dish
Plate the carrot in the centre of the plate. Dress the salmon with sesame oil dressing. Place the salmon on top of the carrots and sprinkle with sesame seeds. Carefully top with the rice. Arrange the other elements as shown, finishing with a *quenelle* of wasabi ice cream.

(see glossary)

BRAISED HOGGET SHOULDER WITH LETTUCE & PEAS

James Chapman, The Scran & Scallie
1 Comely Bank Road, Edinburgh, EH4 1DT
0131 332 6281 www.scranandscallie.com Twitter: @ScranandScallie

SERVES 4

'Velvet' Gerhard Pittnauer, Burgenland, NV (Austria)

Ingredients

Braised Hogget Shoulder

1kg hogget shoulder (buy tied from your butcher)
2 carrots (chopped)
1 onion (chopped)
2 sticks celery (chopped)
½ head garlic
1 tsp peppercorns
1 bouquet garni
1 tsp fennel seeds
2 tsp cumin powder
2 tbsp tomato purée
400ml white wine
1 litre lamb or chicken stock
1 tbsp parsley (chopped)
1 tsp rosemary (chopped)
100g caul fat

Peas A La Française

½ white onion (finely chopped)
90g unsalted butter
1 tbsp salt
600g fresh or frozen peas (podded weight)
100ml whipping cream
10g pancetta (cut into batons)
2 baby gem lettuce (thinly sliced)
salt and pepper

Chef's Tip

Hogget is a hugely underrated ingredient. It is the meat of a young sheep that is older than one year and, as they are a little more mature, you get this great, distinctive and rich flavour, quite different to lamb. Match it with the season's vegetables and you'll make the most of the wonderful flavour.

Method

Braised Hogget Shoulder

Preheat the oven to 160°C.

Heat a heavy bottomed, ovenproof pan, season the hogget shoulder well and colour in the pan until golden all over. Remove from the pan and set aside. Heat the carrots, onions and celery in the same pan and sweat gently for 2-3 minutes. Add the bouquet garni, garlic, peppercorns, fennel seeds and cumin powder. Stir in the tomato purée and sweat for 1-2 minutes, before slowly adding 400ml white wine and cooking off.

Return the shoulder to the pan, pour in the stock and cover with a lid. Place into the oven and leave to cook for 2½-3 hours.

Once cooked, remove the hogget from the stock, open up the hogget shoulder and allow the meat to cool. Meanwhile, pass the stock from the pan through a sieve and reduce it by two thirds. Keep a little bit of the stock aside to use later.

Separate the meat carefully from the shoulder, gently flaking it into a bowl.

Once the stock is reduced, add the flaked meat and season with salt and pepper. Add the parsley and rosemary and mix together.

Form tennis ball sized balls from the hogget mix and wrap in the caul fat. Place the hogget parcels into the stock and baste through for 5-10 minutes over a gentle heat.

For The Peas A La Française

Sweat the onion in 50g of the butter for 4-5 minutes.

Bring a pan of water to the boil and add 1 tablespoon of salt. *Blanch* the peas for 1-2 minutes and refresh in ice water. Drain, then add about one third of the peas (about 200g) to the onions - keep the rest for the finished dish.

Add the cream and seasoning to the peas and onions and cook together for a further 2 minutes.

Blitz quickly and leave to chill – this helps keep the purée green until ready to serve.

To Finish The Peas

Blanch the pancetta in boiling water for 1 minute, then drain through a sieve.

Sweat the bacon in the remaining 40g of butter, then add the rest of peas and pea purée and cook for 3-4 minutes. Add the lettuce and check the seasoning.

To Serve

Serve in a warmed bowl as pictured.

(see glossary)

SEA BUCKTHORN & YOGHURT PANNA COTTA

Tom Kitchin, The Kitchin

78 Commercial Quay, Leith, Edinburgh EH6 6LX.
0131 555 1755 www.thekitchin.com Twitter: @TomKitchin

SERVES 4-6

 *Tokaji Aszu 5 Puttonyos Disznókö, 2006 (Hungary)*

Ingredients

Yoghurt Panna Cotta
125ml double cream
125g yoghurt, 60g caster sugar
2½ leaves bronze gelatine (soaked in water)

Sea Buckthorn Consommé
100g sea buckthorn juice
100ml stock syrup
lemon juice (to taste)

Sea Buckthorn Jelly
142ml sea buckthorn consommé
1½ leaves gelatine (soaked in water until soft)

Apple Balls
2 Granny Smith apples (peeled)
1 lemon (juice of), 50ml stock syrup
10ml calvados

Orange Confit
2 oranges (skin of, white removed)
200ml stock syrup, 1 orange (juice of)

Apple Crisps
1 Granny Smith apple (thinly sliced)
30ml stock syrup, ½ lemon (juice of)

Apple Sorbet
1 litre freshly pressed apple juice
1 lemon (juice of), 1 tsp icing sugar

Meringue
6 large egg whites
1½ tsp white wine vinegar
250g caster sugar, 1 tsp cornflour
1 tsp cornflour (sifted)

To Serve
remaining sea buckthorn consommé

4-6 panna cotta moulds

Method

For The Yoghurt Panna Cotta

Warm the cream and sugar in a heavy bottomed pan over a low heat until the sugar dissolves. Stir in the gelatine before adding the yoghurt. Whisk together until smooth.

For The Sea Buckthorn Consommé

Mix the syrup with the sea buckthorn juice. Add the lemon juice to taste and if needed, more of the stock syrup (at The Kitchin less stock syrup is used to keep a more acidic flavour). Chill.

For The Sea Buckthorn Jelly

Warm half of the consommé and add the gelatine leaves. Once the leaves have dissolved, add the rest of the consommé.

To Build The Panna Cotta

Alternate layers of panna cotta and jelly in your moulds, allowing to set for 45 minutes between layers. Keep chilled.

For The Apple Balls

Ball the apples using a Parisiènne scoop. Combine the stock syrup, lemon juice and calvados. Carefully set the balls into the combined liquids. Set aside.

For The Orange Confit

Cut the skin into triangles. *Blanch* 3 times, then cook in the syrup and juice until softened.

Apple Crisps (Prepare the day before)

Soak the apple slices in the lemon juice and stock syrup before placing on a large, flat baking tray.
Dry in the oven overnight at 60°C, or at 80°C for 3 hours.

For The Apple Sorbet

Combine all the ingredients. Divide into shallow plastic tubs and freeze, churning with a fork every hour until completely frozen.

For The Meringue

Heat the oven to 100°C. Whisk the egg white with the vinegar until they begin to increase in volume. Whisk in two thirds of the sugar, a little at a time. When stiff peaks form, fold in the remaining sugar and cornflour. Transfer to a piping bag and pipe small kisses onto a lined oven tray. Bake for 35-45 minutes, turn off the oven, open the door and leave the tray inside until cool.

To Serve

Serve as pictured.

(see glossary)

MICHELIN STAR SPOTLIGHT...

PAUL KITCHING

HEAD CHEF & OWNER, 21212

I used to visit other chefs in Edinburgh and always think how lucky they were to get the chance to cook and live here. It was this, amongst other things, which made me move to Edinburgh. I think it's the nicest, lightest, freshest, prettiest city in the world and I'm lucky to be able to call it home.

With the wide food offering available in Edinburgh, I regularly eat out. After all, why wouldn't I? The variety of food is only made better by the arts and political scene of the city.

In the restaurant, I like to keep the menu fresh, so I change it around each week, with a heavy influence from the changing seasons. I like to showcase the very best of what this country has to offer in all of my dishes and to do this, I take full advantage of the exceptional, local producers I'm lucky to have right on my doorstep.

As a wee nation, food is at the top of what we do in Scotland. Our smoked salmon is beyond words, our haggis is unbeatable and our root veg is as good as anywhere in the western world. We make the best whisky, great beer, lovely baby vegetables, herbs and mushrooms. Scotland has grown very quickly in the past 20 years in terms of food and for me; we have one of the strongest food identities in the world. We're very protective and proud of our produce, and quite rightly so.

3 Royal Terrace , Edinburgh, EH7 5AB.
0131 523 1030 www.21212restaurant.co.uk

166
MAR HALL GOLF & SPA RESORT

Earl of Mar Estate, Earl of Mar Drive, Bishopton, Renfrewshire, PA7 5NW

0141 812 9999
www.marhall.com Twitter: @MarResort Facebook: marhallresort

Established as a 'must visit' destination for foodies across Scotland and beyond, Mar Hall Golf and Spa Resort is one of the finest and most extensive mansions in Scotland, designed by Sir Robert Smirke. It occupies a very picturesque location on the banks of the River Clyde set within a 240-acre estate. Building began in 1828, with a quarry on the Mar Estate providing the stone, whilst the oak used was specially imported from Canada. Construction was not completed until 1845, with the final bill coming to over £50,000, £2.5m in today's money. The building is erected in the Manorial Gothic Style of Queen Elizabeth I. The splendid irregularity of this style of building has been seldom displayed in modern times. Many of the original features are retained today and it stands firm as one of Scotland's most luxurious 5 star hotels. As well as hosting a championship golf course, a luxury Decleor Spa and 53 individually designed bedrooms, Mar Hall is home to executive chef Jonny MacCallum and head chef Ian McAdams' kitchen.

The Cristal Restaurant offers both an á la carte and a daily market menu. The market menu changes constantly, driven by the availability of local and seasonal produce, while the á la carte depends on seasonal variations. Dishes such as 'Assiette of west coast seafood with citrus salad and goat's cheese panna cotta, pickled baby vegetables and garden herb salad' would be a typical, daily market offering.

Jonny has worked in some notable kitchens across Scotland and Ian spent his last five years at the Auchrannie resort in Arran. This has garnered them both valuable experience which has inspired many dishes. Their combined efforts and passion won the restaurant the accolade of 'Best Hotel Restaurant' Glasgow and Clyde Valley, at the Scottish Hotel Awards.

SCOTTISH LOBSTER & SALMON RAVIOLI, SEARED KING SCALLOPS, BISQUE FOAM, PEA PUREE

SERVES 4

Chardonnay Reserva Terrazas, 2012 (Argentina)

Ingredients

Pasta Dough

250g 00 flour
2 egg yolks
3 whole eggs
2 tsp olive oil

Ravioli Filling

1 Scottish lobster
100g salmon
1 medium egg
20g dill (chopped)
1 lemon (zest of)
salt (to season)
1 egg (beaten, to eggwash)

Scallops

8 king scallops
10g butter
½ lemon (juice of)

Pea Purée

200g peas
100ml cream
½ lemon (juice of)
salt (to season)

Bisque Foam

1 Scottish lobster shell
30g tomato purée
1 white onion (diced)
100ml brandy
300ml water
20ml raspberry vinegar
1 tbsp lecithin
1 lemon (juice of)

Method

For The Pasta Dough

Pulse together the flour and oil in a food processor, then add the eggs and yolks and pulse until the mixture comes together to form a smooth dough. Rest in the fridge for 1 hour.

For The Ravioli Filling

Blanch the lobster for 20 seconds and cool in ice water. Remove all the meat and set aside. Save the shells for the bisque. Separately, blend the salmon, dill and egg to a smooth mousse. Season with salt and the lemon zest. Dice the lobster meat and bind with the salmon mixture.

Chef's Tip

When making your ravioli filling, don't add too much salmon mixture, just enough to hold the diced lobster meat. Be generous with the lobster.

To Prepare The Scallops

Remove the muscle and sinew and set aside on a dry cloth.

For The Pea Purée

Bring the cream to the boil. Add the peas and cook for 1 minute. Blend until smooth with the lemon juice and salt.

For The Bisque Foam

Roast the lobster shells, onions and tomato purée in a pot. Add the brandy and water. Simmer for 20 minutes. Pass through a fine sieve and leave to cool. Whisk together with the raspberry vinegar, lemon juice and lecithin.

To Make The Ravioli

Roll out the pasta thinly using a pasta machine. Cut into eight 8cm rounds. Place a ball of filling on the half rounds and eggwash the edges. Place a round on top and seal the parcels.

To Serve

Boil the ravioli for 3 minutes in seasoned water. Pan sear the scallops on one side for 2 minutes, then turn over and add the butter and lemon juice to finish. Using a dry cloth, drain the ravioli and scallops before assembling on a plate as pictured.

(see glossary)

ROAST LOIN OF SCOTTISH LAMB, WILD MUSHROOM & SPINACH ROSTI, BUTTERNUT SQUASH PUREE, CONFIT CHERRY TOMATOES

SERVES 4

Pinot Noir Cloudy Bay, 2011 (New Zealand)

Ingredients

Lamb

4 x 180g pieces lamb loin
250g dry breadcrumbs
60g parsley (chopped)
30g dill (chopped), 30g mint (chopped)
15ml oil, 10g butter

Wild Mushroom And Spinach Rosti

6 large rooster potatoes (grated)
100g butter (melted)
300g mixed wild mushrooms (cooked)
100g spinach (*blanched)*
2 medium eggs (beaten)

Sauce

1kg lamb bones
75g each carrot, leek, onion (diced)
50g tomato purée
100ml red wine, 75ml port
700ml chicken stock
200ml beef stock

Butternut Squash Purée

1 large butternut squash (diced)
2 stalks rosemary, 3 cloves garlic
50ml water (may not be required)

Confit Cherry Tomatoes

8 cherry tomatoes
4 sprigs thyme (picked)
2 cloves garlic (chopped), 10g sugar
10g salt, 10ml olive oil

Garnish (optional)

4 baby navets (boiled in seasoned water until soft)

Method

For The Wild Mushroom And Spinach Rosti

Preheat the oven to 180°C (fan).

Mix the grated potato and melted butter together and season. Split in two and fry each batch in separate small pans, packed tightly, until golden brown. Layer the spinach on 1 rosti and top with the mushrooms. Add the beaten egg and sandwich the rosti together. Bake for 20 minutes. Press between 2 boards and chill for 2 hours. Cut into 2cm x 10cm rectangles.

For The Sauce

Preheat the oven to 180°C (fan)

Roast the bones for 30 minutes, or until golden.

Roast the vegetables with the tomato purée in a large pan, then add the roasted bones. Cover with stock and alcohol, then simmer for 30 minutes. Pass through a fine sieve, then reduce until thick and glossy.

For The Butternut Squash Purée

Preheat the oven to 180°C (fan).

Place the squash on an oven tray with the rosemary and garlic, cover with foil and bake for 10 minutes or until soft. Blend until smooth, adding a little water if needed. Season with salt.

Chef's Tip

We use a thermomix to get an extremely smooth purée. It's worth the investment.

For The Confit Cherry Tomatoes

Preheat the oven to 70°C (fan).

Blanch the tomatoes for 10 seconds, then cool in ice water. Peel off the skins, then sprinkle the tomatoes with the herbs, oil, garlic, sugar and salt. Bake for 35 minutes.

For The Lamb

Preheat the oven to 180°C (fan).

Season the lamb with salt before searing in a hot pan. Place in the oven for 4-6 minutes. Allow to rest for 10 minutes.

Blend the breadcrumbs with the herbs and oil, brush the mix onto the lamb.

To Serve

Warm the rosti, cherry tomatoes and lamb under a grill. Assemble the elements of the dish as pictured.

(see glossary)

CRANACHAN SOUFFLE WITH HEATHER HONEY ICE CREAM

SERVES 4

 *Muscat De Beaumes-De-Venise les Trois Fonte, 2008 (France)*

Ingredients

Heather Honey Ice cream

200ml milk
100ml double cream
1 vanilla pod
50g egg yolks
75g caster sugar
50g heather honey

Crème Pâtissière

450ml milk
100ml Drambuie
6 egg yolks
125g caster sugar
40g flour
15g cornflour
100g raspberries

Soufflé

90g egg whites
40g caster sugar
150g crème pâtissière
icing sugar (to dust)

To Prepare The Ramekins

30g oats (toasted)
20g butter (softened)

Method

To Prepare The Ramekins

Cover the inside of 4 ramekins with softened butter. Toss the toasted oats around the butter until evenly covered.

For The Heather Honey Ice Cream (Prepare ahead)

Pour the milk, cream and vanilla pod into a pan and bring to the boil. Whisk the egg yolks and sugar until pale, then pour over the hot mixture. Whisk in the honey and continue to cook until it has the consistency of custard. Pass through a sieve, chill, then churn in an ice cream machine.

For The Crème Pâtissière

Combine the milk and Drambuie and bring to the boil. Whisk together the yolks, sugar and flours. Stir in the raspberries before pouring over the hot liquid. Continue to cook for 2-3 minutes until very thick. Cover and chill.

For The Soufflé

Preheat the oven to 180°C (fan).

Whisk the egg whites, slowly adding the caster sugar, until the mixture holds firm peaks. Whisk half of the egg mix into the crème pâtissière, then slowly fold in the rest. Spoon the mixture into the ramekins and bake for 12-15 minutes.

Chef's Tip

Keep your oven door closed when cooking soufflé. Don't be tempted to peak, or they could collapse.

To Serve

Simply scoop the ice cream onto a plate. Holding each ramekin with a napkin, dust the soufflé with icing sugar as soon as they come out of the oven and enjoy!

176
MHOR 84 MOTEL

Balquhidder, Lochearnhead, Perthshire, FK19 8NY

01877 384 646
www.mhor.net/mhor84-motel Twitter: @MHOR84 Facebook: Mhor 84 Motel

otel Mhor 84 is currently the final piece in the Mhor jigsaw. The story began back in 1983 when the Lewis family moved to Monachyle Mhor. Originally it was run as a family farm with Scottish black-face sheep and cattle.

In 2013 Tom and Lisa Lewis joined forces with brother Dick Lewis and Mhairi Taylor (of Delizique, Glasgow's west end) to create the perfect pit stop on the A84 at the head of Balquhidder Glen. They have created an affordable motel and restaurant serving food from 8am-9pm every day. The same principles as Monachyle Mhor are followed through in the restaurant, using seasonal and local produce, but in a more informal environment.

Prior to Mhor 84, other Mhor ventures include Mhor Fish, established in 2005 and Mhor Bread in 2006. Both of these businesses owned by Tom and Dick, are based in Callander.

Although Mhor Fish has only been in existence for 10 years, the site has been operating for 100 years. Since the Lewis's changed the name, the business has gone full circle from just providing fish and chips, to becoming a fresh fish retailer, to the present day when Mhor Fish has now gone back to its roots and concentrates on great quality fish and chips and changing daily specials.

They pride themselves in knowing the source of their fish, down to the individual boats, the types of net used and when the catch was landed.

Mhor Bread has been operating for nine years but similarly, the bakery has been baking bread in Callander for over 100 years. It provides fresh bread to the community, only ever closing at Christmas and New Year. The only ingredients in their breads are flour, water and salt. All the meat for the pies is sourced from local cattle and when available, they use mutton in their traditional Scotch pies.

MHOR
MURRAY'S ALES
PUBLIC BAR

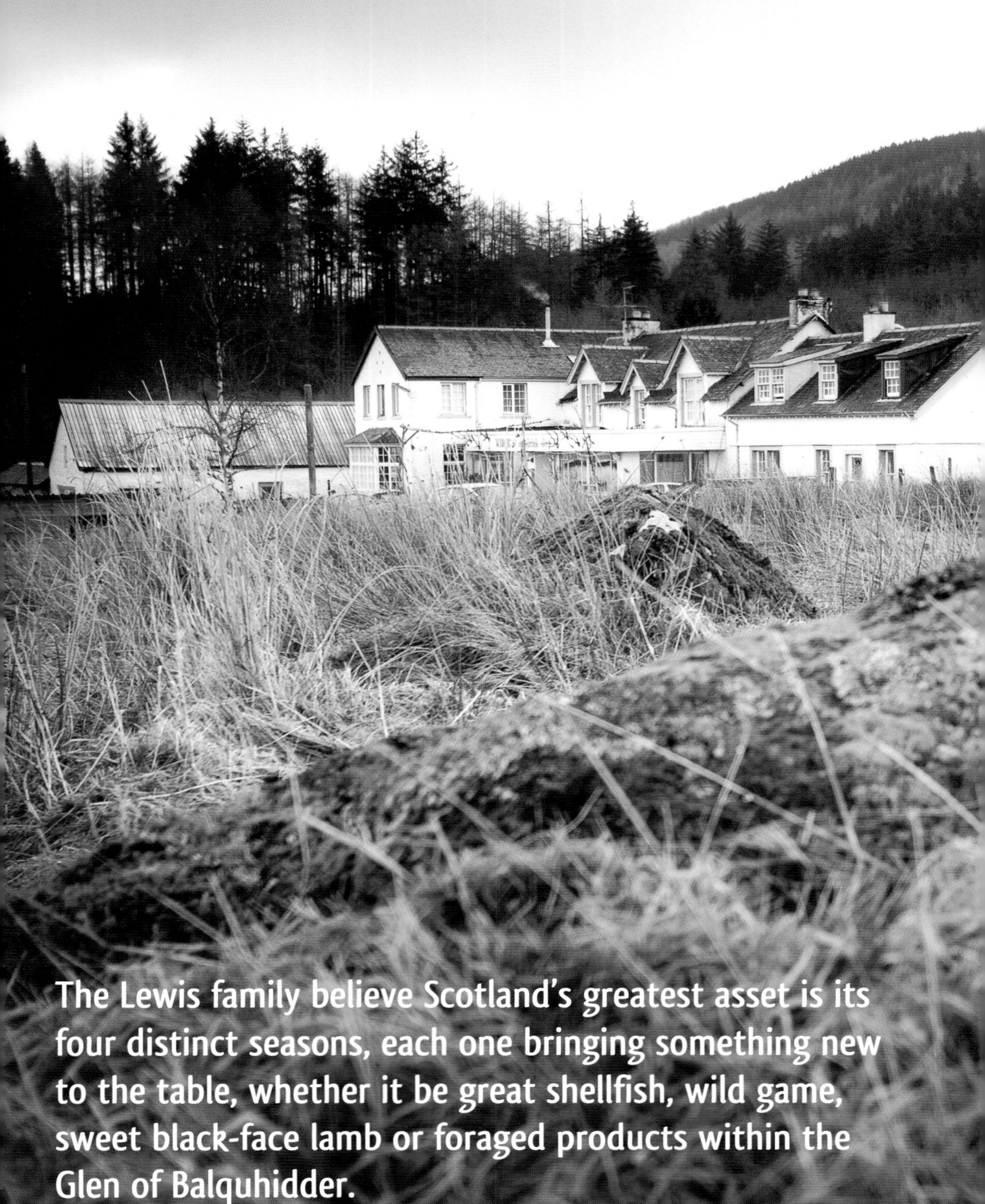

The Lewis family believe Scotland's greatest asset is its four distinct seasons, each one bringing something new to the table, whether it be great shellfish, wild game, sweet black-face lamb or foraged products within the Glen of Balquhidder.

SHETLAND SALMON, BEETROOT SLAW, HORSERADISH CREME FRAICHE, ROASTED ALMONDS

SERVES 4

Glengoyne
12 Year Old

Ingredients

Salmon

320g salmon (centre cut, skin-on)
½ lemon (juice of)
butter (knob of)

Beetroot Slaw

2 large raw beetroots (peeled, grated)
2 red onions (thinly sliced)
2 tbsp Maldon sea salt
fennel seeds (pinch of, lightly crushed, toasted)
3 tbsp mayonnaise
1 heaped tbsp English mustard
tarragon (handful of, chopped)
2 Braeburn apples (cut into batons)

Horseradish Crème Fraîche

200g Katy Rogers crème fraîche (the best there is!)
50g creamed horseradish
1 lemon (zest of)
salt and pepper (to taste)
1 tbsp dill (chopped)

Roasted Almonds

100g blanched almonds
1 shallot (finely chopped)
2 tbsp sherry vinegar
40ml Summer Harvest rapeseed oil
1 tbsp parsley (chopped)
½ lemon (juice of)

To Serve

wilted spinach

Method

For The Beetroot Slaw

Mix the grated beetroot and onion together. Season with salt. Leave for 10 minutes for the vegetables to soften. Strain through a colander. Rinse for 1 minute, then squeeze off any excess moisture.

Place the mixture into a mixing bowl and combine all the ingredients. Fold through gently and season to taste.

For The Horseradish Crème Fraîche

Mix all the ingredients together then put it in the fridge to firm up for 30 minutes.

For The Roasted Almonds

Roast the almonds until golden brown. Lightly crush them, then mix all of the ingredients together. Season to taste.

For The Salmon

Cut the salmon into 4 pieces and lightly oil the skin-side.

Heat a non-stick pan and place the salmon in, skin-side down. Cook for 1-2 minutes until the skin is golden brown and crispy. Turn the fish over and cook for a further 2 minutes.

Add a knob of butter and a squeeze of ½ lemon. Once the butter starts to foam, baste the salmon for 30 seconds. Rest for 1 minute before plating.

Chef's Tip

Always remember that the fish will continue to cook at the table with the residual heat.

To Serve

Serve as pictured.

GARETH'S BEEF BURGER WITH CHIPOTLE KETCHUP

SERVES 4

½ Pint of West Beer with a 15 Year Old Glengoyne – 'Half and a Half'!

Ingredients

Gareth's Beef Burger

500g beef mince
1 small red onion (diced)
½ white onion (diced)
few sprigs thyme (chopped)
2 tbsp tomato paste
1 tbsp English mustard
2 cloves garlic (grated)
parsley (handful of, chopped)
1 egg
20g breadcrumbs
salt and pepper
Tabasco (dash of)

Chipotle Ketchup

500g plum vine tomatoes
1 chipotle dried chilli
20g smoked Maldon salt
20g smoked paprika
2 pears (peeled, cored, roughly chopped)
1 large white onion (roughly chopped)
4 cloves garlic (chopped)
175ml cider vinegar
125g light muscovado sugar
50ml Summer Harvest rapeseed oil

Jean's Dark Beer Bread

450g strong white flour
450g wholemeal seeded flour
25g salt
rapeseed oil (splash of)
20g fresh yeast (ask politely at your local bakers!)
1 tsp honey
320ml warm water, 300ml dark beer

To Serve

tomatoes (sliced)
gherkins (sliced)
red cabbage (shredded)
cheese
iceberg lettuce

Method

For Gareth's Beef Burger

Mix all the ingredients together and taste to check seasoning. Divide the mix into 4 even patties and place in the fridge for about 1 hour to firm up.

Preheat the oven to 180°C (fan).

Very lightly oil the burgers on both sides. Add the patties to a medium to hot frying pan and colour on both sides. Transfer to a hot oven for 6 minutes.

Chef's Tip
Don't overwork the meat.

For The Chipotle Ketchup (Prepare ahead, makes a 500ml jar)

Heat the rapeseed oil in a large pot on a medium heat.

Mix all of the ingredients together, apart from the sugar, and add to the pot.

Gently simmer for 2 hours, stirring occasionally to stop it catching. Take off the heat and blitz until smooth.

Transfer into a clean pot and add the sugar. Simmer for 30 minutes, then leave to cool. Store in the fridge in a sterilised jar.

To Make Jean's Dark Beer Bread

Place the flours into a big bowl, add the salt and rapeseed oil.

Mix 100ml of the warm water with the yeast and honey. As soon as it starts to bubble add it to the flour and mix together. Slowly add the rest of the water and the beer to the flour mix, little by little, until it all comes together as a dough but is still tacky to the touch. You may not need all of the water or you may need a touch more, see how the dough feels.

Remove the dough from the bowl and place on a lightly floured worktop. Knead it for a couple of minutes until it starts to feel slightly elastic. At this point you may need to add a touch more water. Knead the dough to a count of 50. You should be able to stretch the dough.

Cover with a cloth and set aside in a warm place for 40-60 minutes.

Preheat the oven to 200°C.

Take the dough out of the bowl and mould into your desired shape. Leave to prove again in a warm place for another 20 minutes or so.

Bake in the oven for 20-40 minutes, dependent on the size of the loaf or buns.

You know when it's ready if you tap the bottom of the bread and it sounds hollow. Place on a cooling rack.

To Serve

Serve as pictured

TREACLE TART WITH CLOTTED CREAM & CANDIED ORANGE

SERVES 4

Deanston
12 Year Old

Ingredients

Pastry

125g unsalted butter (softened)
100g icing sugar
250g plain flour (sifted)
50g ground almonds
1 orange (zest of)
salt (pinch of)
2 large eggs (lightly beaten)

Treacle Filling

220g butter
500g golden syrup
175g treacle
180g wholemeal sourdough breadcrumbs
75ml double cream
2 eggs
1 egg yolk
salt (pinch of)

Candied Orange Peel

1 orange
500ml sugar syrup
200g caster sugar

To Serve

clotted cream

Method

For The Pastry

Cream together the butter and sugar. Fold in the flour, ground almonds and salt. Add the eggs to form a dough. Wrap in cling film and rest in the fridge for about an hour or more.

Preheat the oven to 160°C (fan).

Roll the pastry out to 3mm thick. Line the pastry case and blind bake for 30 minutes. Remove the baking beans and cook for a further 10 minutes, until the pastry is crisp and golden.

For The Treacle Filling

Melt the butter over a medium heat until it turns golden brown. Mix in the golden syrup and treacle, then remove from the heat. Pass the mixture through a sieve to remove any solids, then set aside.

Mix the sourdough crumbs in a bowl with the butter and treacle mix. Whisk all the other ingredients in and leave to cool for 15 minutes. Pour into the tart case and cook for a further 40 minutes at 140°C (fan). Serve at room temperature.

For The Candied Orange Peel

Peel the orange and remove any pith. Shred the peel finely and add to the sugar syrup. Simmer for 30 minutes, then strain and toss in the caster sugar while still warm.

To Serve

Serve as pictured.

Chef's Tip

This is a favourite of all the staff at Mhor. Don't be tempted to nibble on it before you serve it - or there may be none left!

MICHELIN STAR SPOTLIGHT...

CHARLIE LOCKLEY

HEAD CHEF/DIRECTOR, BOATH HOUSE

I have been head chef at Boath House, Nairn, for the past 18 years, and I am delighted to hold a coveted Michelin Star, 4 AA Rosettes and title of Scottish Chef of the Year. This puts our restaurant firmly in the top four restaurants in Scotland and as one of the most notable in Britain.

I had never planned to become a chef - my ambition was to become a blacksmith! In 1984, after a bit of travelling and working my way up the ranks in the kitchens (initially for beer money), including a stint at Nico's 90 Park Lane, I started to really enjoy the buzz and the satisfaction of seeing people enjoy the food I had created.

It was chef Nico Ladenis' book 'My Gastronomy' that really inspired me. It demonstrated that with sheer determination and passion, you can achieve your dreams at any age. My food is about the marriage of pure flavour combinations and uncomplicated preparation. Let the ingredients do the talking.

More than ten years later, in 1997, I heard a rumour that a couple, Wendy and Don Matheson, were renovating a Georgian mansion close to where I lived. They had the same ideas, passion and dreams as me, and the rest is history... Boath House was born. With 4 AA Rosettes and a Michelin star under our belt, we continue to strive to better ourselves and to keep our customers happy. Stagnancy is not an option! Seasonality is!

Wendy designs the garden bearing a fruit orchard and two poly tunnels. There is a bounty of foraged and organically grown food from the 20 acre estate and the large Victorian, walled kitchen garden at Boath. The greenhouse keeps the kitchen supplied all year round with rare micro herbs, fruit, vegetables and wild flowers.

Nairnshire's local producers and suppliers are wonderful; with lamb from Peter Muskus, beef from Macbeth's, shellfish from Keltic Seafare and cheeses from Conage Dairy to name just a few.

Wendy, Don and I pride ourselves on our association with and involvement in Slow Food and organic cooking. I was delighted to recently be one of only a small number of UK chefs invited to Terra Madre, Italy and attend the bi-annual Salone del Gusto in Turin, by the Slow Food Association as the Highlands Convivial representative.

The restaurant serves a daily changing menu from which you can choose between three to six courses, showcasing the best of the local, natural larder. Service in the restaurant is attentive yet relatively informal.

Boath House Hotel, Auldearn, Nairn, IV12 5TE.
01667 454896 www.boath-house.com

188 MONACHYLE MHOR HOTEL

Balquhidder, Lochearnhead, Perthshire, FK19 8PQ

01877 384 622
www.mhor.net/monachyle-mhor-hotel Twitter: @MhorHotel Facebook: Monachyle Mhor Hotel

Monachyle Mhor Hotel was originally founded by Tom Lewis' parents Rob and Jean. When Jean wanted to buy a bicycle for Tom's brother Dick, she put a sign on the side of the road advertising soup and sandwiches to pay for the bike. Monachyle Mhor has since evolved into a fully licensed hotel and restaurant, which is situated six miles down a single track road in Balquhidder. The farm supplies as much beef, lamb, pork and game as they can produce. The kitchen garden also produces an abundance of vegetables, salads, soft fruit, apples and pears.

Tom Lewis took over all of the day-to-day cooking at Monachyle Mhor in 1996 and the business started to expand with the help of his wife Lisa and brother Dick. Monachyle Mhor is a regular pilgrimage site for Scottish foodies and the hotel sits in a remote scenic spot overlooking Loch Voil in the Trossachs. Tom and the Lewis family's aim is to provide the finest Scottish food and hospitality in the most beautiful surroundings.

MHOR photography: Melanie Lewis

A vibrant splash of pink against the surrounding mountains, this 18th Century farmhouse and steadings is now a cosy boutique hotel and restaurant with 14 individually designed rooms.

HAND DIVED MULL SCALLOP, DRESSED CRAB & GARDEN LEEK

SERVES 4

Glengoyne 12 Year Old

Ingredients

Hand Dived Mull Scallops

4 hand dived Mull scallops
2 tbsp olive oil
1 tbsp lemon juice
salt and pepper
butter (knob of)

Dressed Crab

2 crabs (picked white crab meat)
1 shallot (finely chopped)
1 tbsp tarragon (finely chopped)
2 tbsp parsley (finely chopped)
½ Granny Smith apple (finely diced)
1 tsp Dijon mustard
1 lemon (juice of)
½ lemon (zest of)
2 tbsp Katy Rogers crème fraîche
salt and pepper (to taste)

Garden Leeks

4 baby garden leeks
100g fresh garden peas (shelled)
salt and pepper (to taste)
vinaigrette (splash of)

Chilli, Ginger And Coriander Dressing

1 red chilli (deseeded, finely chopped)
½ banana shallot (finely chopped)
1cm fresh ginger (peeled, finely chopped)
2 tbsp coriander (finely chopped)
1 lime (juice of)
3-4 tbsp rapeseed oil
salt and pepper (to taste)

Garnish

coriander leaves

Method

For The Chilli, Ginger And Coriander Dressing

Mix all ingredients together and season well.

For The Hand Dived Mull Scallops

Season the scallops well with salt and pepper. Place them in a pan and cook for 2 minutes, until starting to turn golden. Turn them over, squeeze over the lemon juice and add a knob of butter.

Cook for another minute.

Chef's Tip

Always use hand dived scallops.

For The Dressed Crab

Put all ingredients in mixing bowl and fold together. Season with salt and pepper to taste. Place in the fridge until you're ready to serve.

For The Garden Leeks

Blanch the leeks and peas in boiling water. Place in a pan with a splash of vinaigrette. Season well, and wilt for another 30 seconds.

To Serve

Serve as pictured, garnished with fresh coriander leaf.

(see glossary)

MONACHYLE VENISON, GARDEN CHARD & BALQUHIDDER CHANTERELLES

SERVES 4

Glengoyne 15 Year Old
The sweetness of the venison and the earthiness of the chanterelles makes it the perfect combination.

Ingredients

Venison

1-1½kg venison haunch (seam trimmed)
butter (knob of)
salt and pepper

Roast Shallot And Garlic Purée

3 cloves garlic (unpeeled)
1 sprig thyme
12 whole shallots (unpeeled)
2 tsp sea salt flakes
1 tsp freshly ground black pepper
2 tbsp olive oil
50ml double cream

Garden Vegetables

4-6 rainbow pink chard leaves (washed)
2-4 runner beans (washed, cut evenly)
4-6 carrots (peeled, halved)
4-6 turnips (peeled, halved)
butter (knob of)
salt and pepper

Balquhidder Chanterelles

150g chanterelles
butter (knob of)
salt and pepper
1 tbsp parsley (chopped)
3 leaves tarragon
1 sprig parsley
½ lemon (squeeze of)

Method

For The Venison Haunch

Preheat the oven to 210°C (fan).

Season the venison well.

Heat a frying pan, add the knob of butter and pan fry the venison quickly, until coloured on all sides.

Place the venison in the oven for 4-7 minutes, depending on the size. Remove and transfer to a warm plate to rest for 5 minutes. Reduce the juices in the pan to make a jus.

Chef's Tip

Use the freshest venison from Scotland to get the best flavour.

For The Roast Shallot And Garlic Purée

Preheat oven to 180°C (fan).

Place the garlic, thyme and shallots in a small baking dish. Sprinkle with salt, pepper and olive oil, cover with foil and bake until soft, for about 30 minutes. Leave to cool to room temperature.

Peel the garlic and shallots, then purée in a food processor with the double cream. Keep hot.

For The Garden Vegetables

Blanch the carrots, runner beans and turnips in boiling salted water until tender, but still crunchy. Place in iced water to refresh.

Warm a pan, on a medium heat, and melt the butter. Add the *blanched* garden vegetables and chard leaves. Wilt for a minute, season well with salt and pepper. Serve immediately.

For The Balquhidder Chanterelles

Clean the mushrooms with a pastry brush. Heat a pan on a medium to hot heat, add a knob of butter, then the chanterelles. Season with salt and pepper. Add the chopped parsley and tarragon.

Spritz with a squeeze of lemon juice.

To Serve

Serve as pictured.

(see glossary)

WARM BRAMBLES WITH BROWN BREAD ICE CREAM, HEATHER HONEY SOURDOUGH CRISP

SERVES 8

Glengoyne
18 Year Old

Ingredients

Brown Bread Ice Cream

1 loaf brown bread
6 tsp ground cinnamon
8 tbsp Demerara sugar
500ml full-fat milk
500ml double cream
1 vanilla pod (split in half, scraped)
2 tbsp heather honey
12 egg yolks
150g caster sugar
1-2 lemons (juice of, to taste)

Heather Honey Sourdough Crisp

¼ sourdough loaf (partially frozen)
2 tbsp heather honey

Warm Brambles

400g brambles
1 tbsp heather honey
lemon juice (squeeze of)
1 tsp sugar

Method

For The Brown Bread Ice Cream (Prepare ahead)

Preheat the oven to 180°C (fan).

Crumble half the loaf of bread. Mix with half the cinnamon and 5 tablespoons of Demerara. Toast in the oven for 15 minutes. Pour the milk and cream over the toasted bread and leave for 1 hour to infuse.

Strain the mixture, add the heather honey and vanilla and bring gradually to the boil.

Whisk the egg yolks and caster sugar until pale white. Pour a little of the heated cream into the egg yolks, then pour back into the pan. Whisk constantly until the mixture coats the back of the spoon. Leave to cool.

Remove the middle/soft part from the other half of the bread and place in the blender. Blitz with the rest of the cinnamon and sugar until it reaches a fine crumb. Place in the oven for 15-20 minutes until crispy and golden in colour. Add the lemon juice to your taste, to the ice cream base. Churn in an ice cream machine until the ice cream becomes soft in texture, then add the brown breadcrumbs and finish churning the ice cream. Place in the freezer.

For The Heather Honey Sourdough Crisp

Preheat oven to 200°C (fan).

Thinly slice the sourdough loaf and place on a flat baking tray with a silicon mat. Using a pastry brush, paint the honey all over the sourdough slices. Bake in the oven for 10-15 minutes until golden brown.

Remove from the tray and place on a cooling rack.

For The Warm Brambles

Preheat oven to 200°C (fan).

Put everything into a pan and place into the oven for 5 minutes. Finish the brambles with a splash of your favourite malt whisky when they come out of the oven.

Chef's Tip

Don't overcook the brambles. Warm them through, don't cook them.

To Serve

Serve as pictured.

MOONFISH CAFE

9 Correction Wynd, Aberdeen, AB10 1HP

01224 644 166
www.moonfishcafe.co.uk Twitter: @moonfishcafe Facebook: Moonfish Cafe

Established in 2004 by Christian Recomio, and now joined by Brian McLeish, Moonfish Café leads the city's food scene. The restaurant is located on the medieval streets of Aberdeen's Merchant Quarter with views of the 12th Century Kirk of St Nicholas, and has been serving diners consistent, uncomplicated food for more than a decade. The kitchen's constantly changing, innovative menus reflect the seasons and some of the best produce the UK has to offer. The front of house team delivers effortless and simple service with a nod to natural and small batch produced wines and an extensive gin list.

Brian trained with Paul Hart at The Old Course Hotel in St Andrews before moving to Ireland to work in the award-winning Tannery Restaurant and Cook School with Paul Flynn. Upon returning to Scotland, Brian became sous chef to Adam Handling at the Fairmont in St Andrews before moving to Aberdeen to take on the head chef job at Moonfish.

Since 2012, with Christian going on to open sister restaurant Sitka in Kuala Lumpur, Brian has elevated the cuisine of Moonfish to a much more British focused menu, resulting in him becoming partner and director.

As well as winning numerous awards, including the Observer Food Monthly Awards Best Runner Up 2011, 2012, 2013 and 2014, along with being included in the Waitrose Good Food Guide 2014, Brian was a finalist in MasterChef: The Professionals 2014.

MOONFISH CAFE
sam brill
ísland

The small team at Moonfish offers casual dining in a relaxed, unpretentious atmosphere.

Villtur skjól tveir

SPICED LAMB BELLY, CARROT, CORIANDER, GHERKIN

SERVES 4

Bodegas y Viñedos Merayo Mencia 2013, Bierzo (Spain). Soft, juicy, racy blueberry fruit.

Ingredients

Spiced Lamb Belly

1kg lamb belly (boneless, skinless)
25g ground cumin
25g ground coriander
10g ground ginger
salt and pepper
100g transglutaminase powder (meat glue)
1 clove garlic
1 large red chilli
100g fresh coriander

Picked Onions

10 silverskin onions
100ml white wine vinegar
125g caster sugar
2 star anise
1 stick cinnamon
6 cloves
50ml beetroot juice

Carrot Purée

500g carrots (peeled, diced)
3 bay leaves
1 star anise
20 pink peppercorns
1 tsp ground ginger
4 cardamom pods (crushed)

Garnish

1 purple carrot
4 good quality gherkins
micro coriander
olive oil

Method

For The Lamb Belly (Prepare the day before)
Trim away any fatty bits left on the belly. Cut into 4 equal size pieces. Place the bellies in a large bowl, add the spices, seasoning and meat glue and mix well to coat each belly in the spices. Stack the bellies on top of each other and place in a vac pack bag. Add the garlic, chilli and coriander to the bag and seal on full pressure. Place in a water bath set at 75°C for 12 hours. Remove from the bath and press the bellies in a fridge overnight. Remove the bellies from the bag, take away the fat and trim the edges. Pan fry to caramelise just before serving.
Alternatively, cook the belly as a terrine in a *bain-marie* at 140°C for 2 hours.

Chef's Tip
If the lamb belly is hard to find, you can substitute for any other cut, but the belly is worth looking for.

For The Pickled Onions (Prepare the day before)
Remove the skin from the onions and cut them in half.
Bring the vinegar to the boil with the sugar and spices, then remove from the heat and add the beetroot juice. Allow to cool. Bring back to the boil, then pass through a sieve to remove the spices. Add the onions to the hot liquid and leave to cool. These are best left overnight to absorb all the flavour and colour.

For The Carrot Purée
Preheat the oven to 80°C.
Place the carrots in an ovenproof dish with the bay leaves and spices. Cover with foil and place in the oven for 20 minutes, or until the carrots are cooked. Remove the star anise and bay leaves from the bowl. Place everything else into a blender and blend until smooth. Pass through a sieve and correct the seasoning. Keep warm.

For The Garnish
Using a *mandolin*, slice the purple carrot as thin as possible. Store in cold water until needed. Slice the gherkins on the *mandolin* too. Pick through the micro coriander to select the best leaves.

To Assemble
Place the lamb belly in the centre of the plate. Dot the carrot purée down one side of the plate. Place 3 pieces of the pickled onion and 4 slices of gherkin around the purée. Drain the purple carrots, drizzle with the olive oil and season. Arrange 5 pieces of carrot on and around the purée. Scatter the micro coriander. The dish should look natural – the garnish does not need to be the same on every plate.

(see glossary)

POACHED HALIBUT, CAULIFLOWER, MUSSELS, SAFFRON, HAZELNUT

SERVES 4

Domaine des Baumard, Savennieres Clos St Yves 2007, Anjou-Saumur (France).
Pure, clean fresh fruit, mineral, dry and elegant.

Ingredients

Hazelnut Crumb
200g hazelnuts (*blanched*, peeled)
50g chives (finely chopped)

Poached Halibut
4 x 150g halibut fillets (centre cut)
500ml chicken stock
1 bay leaf, 10 white peppercorns
1 sprig rosemary
1 slice smoked pancetta, 1 clove garlic

Cauliflower Purée
250g cauliflower (sliced, leaves discarded)
80ml milk, 80ml double cream
1 sprig thyme, 1 tsp icing sugar
white truffle oil and salt (to season)

Pickled Cauliflower
150g cauliflower (sliced on a *mandolin*)
30g sea salt, 300ml rice wine vinegar
20g caster sugar, 3g lemon zest, 2g table salt

Cauliflower Florets
300g cauliflower (cut into large florets, *blanched*)
olive oil (to fry), 1 clove garlic, 1 sprig thyme
100g unsalted butter
nutmeg (grating of) and salt and pepper (to season)

Spring Onions
12 spring onions (trimmed, outer skin removed)
10ml vegetable oil, salt and pepper

Mussels
1kg mussels (scrubbed, beards removed)
200ml dry white wine, 1 clove garlic (sliced)
1 banana shallot (sliced), 1 bay leaf

Saffron Sauce
200ml reserved mussel stock
4g saffron, 2g orange zest, 100ml milk

Method

For The Hazelnut Crumb
Roast the hazelnuts for 5 minutes (180°C). Cool, then pulse Mix with the chives.

For The Halibut
Simmer the stock with the aromats for 15 minutes. Reduce to a low heat (45°C) and gently cook the fillets until the core temperature is 45°C. Drain on kitchen cloth. Carefully remove the skin, season the fish and spoon the hazelnut crumb on top.

For The Cauliflower Purée
Simmer the cauliflower with the milk, cream, sugar and thyme until tender. Strain the liquid into a clean pan and reduce to a creamy consistency. Remove the thyme and blitz the cauliflower in a blender, adding a little reduced liquid until thick and velvety. Season to taste. Pass through a sieve, keep warm in a squeezy bottle.

For The Pickled Cauliflower
Sprinkle the cauliflower with sea salt and leave for 20 minutes. Rinse and pat dry. Bring the other ingredients to the boil, allow to cool, then pour over the cauliflower. Leave for 1 hour.

For The Cauliflower Florets
Cut each floret in half to leave a flat side. Gently fry, flat side down, in a hot pan with oil until caramelised. Add the other ingredients and allow the butter to foam. Season and drain on kitchen paper.

For The Spring Onions
Blanch the onions in salted, boiling water, and refresh in ice water. Drain and pat dry. Brush the onions with the oil and season. Chargrill to get good markings and a bitter flavour. Drain on kitchen paper.

For The Mussels
Boil the wine with the shallot, garlic and bay leaf. Add the mussels, cover and shake occasionally until the shells have opened, discarding any that don't open. Drain into a colander lined with muslin over a bowl. Keep the cooking liquid for the sauce. Pick the meat from the shells and chill until needed. Gently warm the mussels in some stock before serving.

For The Saffron Sauce
Boil the stock and saffron until reduced by half. Add the milk and zest, bring to the boil, correct the seasoning and foam using a hand blender. Serve the froth from the top of the sauce.

To Serve
Serve as pictured, spooning on the foam just before serving.

(see glossary)

PEAR & ROSEMARY CHEESECAKE

SERVES 6

Grandjó, late harvest, Real Companhia Velha, 2008 (Portugal)
Baked yellow fruit, sultana and citrus, botrytis influenced and perfectly balanced.

Ingredients

Pears

400g caster sugar
18 baby pears
3 large sprigs rosemary

Cream Cheese

500g mascarpone cheese
1 vanilla pod (seeds of)
200g icing sugar
100ml double cream

Peanut Sable

100g salted peanuts
60g unsalted butter
40g caster sugar
1 vanilla pod (seeds of)
2g salt
55g plain flour

Pear Jellies

940ml pear juice
730g caster sugar
30g pectin powder
10g citric acid
100ml spring water
200g liquid glucose
caster sugar (to dust)

Peanut Butter Ganache

1 jar smooth peanut butter
100g icing sugar
1 vanilla pod (seeds of)
50ml double cream

Chocolate Tuile

15g cocoa powder
75g plain flour
75g icing sugar
68ml milk
13g butter (melted)

Method

For The Pears

Place the sugar into a heavy bottomed saucepan and heat until golden. Add the pears and rosemary and cook until the pears are tender. Cool before handling.

For The Cream Cheese

Beat the cream in a food processor. Add the vanilla seeds and sugar and beat until smooth. Slowly add the cream whilst still beating. Store in a clean tub in the fridge.

For The Peanut Sable

Blitz the peanuts in a food processor to a large crumb. Cream the sugar and butter with the vanilla seeds. Mix in the flour, salt and peanuts. When a dough forms, stop beating and leave to rest for 1 hour.

Preheat the oven to 175°C.

Roll the mix out between 2 sheets of greaseproof paper to just over 1cm thick. Cut into rounds and bake in the oven for 12 minutes. Remove from the oven and dust with caster sugar whilst still hot.

For The Pear Jellies

Line a baking tray with cling film.

Bring the pear juice to the boil in a large saucepan. Mix 60g of sugar with the pectin and whisk into the boiling juice. Allow to come back to the boil. Add 670g of sugar and glucose and keep boiling, stirring often until it reaches 107°C.

Dissolve the citric acid in the spring water. Take the saucepan off the heat and mix in the citric acid. Pour the mix into the lined tray and leave to cool to room temperature. Cut the jellies into squares and dust in caster sugar.

For The Peanut Butter Ganache

Place the peanut butter, vanilla seeds and icing sugar in a bowl and beat. Slowly add the cream and combine until smooth. Keep in a piping bag until needed.

For The Chocolate Tuile

Sift the dry ingredients into bowl. Slowly mix in the milk and butter until smooth. Rest in the fridge for 1 hour. Spread out on greaseproof paper as thin as possible. Bake in the oven at 180°C for 6 minutes or until lightly coloured and crisp. Allow to cool, break into pieces.

To Serve

Pipe the ganache on the plate. Arrange the pears next to it and a *quenelle* of cream cheese at the side. Garnish with the jellies, peanut sable crumb and chocolate tuile.

Chef's Tip

This can all be prepped a day before and arranged just before service, which makes it much easier when entertaining.

(see glossary)

MICHELIN STAR SPOTLIGHT...

TONY PIERCE

HEAD CHEF, KNOCKINAAM LODGE

Knockinaam and I came together quite by chance in 1994 and I have been here ever since.

I studied general catering at Salford College, Manchester and after three years as a waiter I applied for a job in the kitchen of the Britannia Hotel. The head chef, Noel Goulding, must have seen some promise as he suggested I try for a position at Gleneagles. The following spring I started and after a year I decided to concentrate on smaller, finer dining restaurants. From Gleneagles I did stints at Mallory Court Hotel, The Box Tree in Ilkley, back to Scotland to Inverlochy Castle and then to Llangeod Hall in Wales.

Travelling from Plymouth to the Isle of Skye to visit my friends, I stopped off at Southwaite Service Station for petrol and decided to go in for some sweets. Having a sneaky read of The Caterer and Hotelkeeper magazine (back then there was no such thing as internet!), my eye caught an advert which advertised 'urgently required chef'. After making a short phone call, I took a sharp left at Carlisle and headed to Knockinaam. I fell in love with the hotel and the beautiful area and subsequently a local girl who I have since married.

My passion is classic French cuisine with the best Scottish ingredients. We try to source as much local produce as possible and our gardener, Sandy Murray, assists with providing a wonderful supply of fresh vegetables, berries and herbs from our kitchen garden throughout the year. Other notable suppliers are Island Divers for first class scallops and langoustines, local fisherman Trevor from Drummore for amazing lobsters, John Mellis in Dumfriesshire for the best honey anywhere and Alex Jack Butchers in Stranraer for being so consistent with our meat supply. Those factors and a great team at the Lodge has helped retain the Michelin star for the last 20 years.

Knockinaam Lodge, Portpatrick, Stranraer, Wigtownshire DG9 9AD.
01776 810471 www.knockinaamlodge.com

210 THE PEAT INN

By St Andrews, Fife, KY15 5LH

01334 840 206
www.thepeatinn.co.uk Twitter: @ThePeatInn Facebook: The Peat Inn Restaurant With Rooms

When chef patron Geoffrey Smeddle and his wife Katherine first moved to The Peat Inn to run their own restaurant, they admit that a big part of the draw was the fabulous location. "The pretty coastal villages scattered along the enchanting shores of the East Neuk remain as picturesque and intriguing to us today as they did a decade ago," said Geoffrey. "The coastal walks and undulating hills sloping down to unspoilt beaches create a sense of space, relaxation and charm which is hard to resist. Our overnight guests certainly seem to agree.

"Over the years it has been our pleasure, and a privilege, to discover a network of outstanding suppliers and local producers who, without doubt, have helped us to earn a Michelin star for the restaurant."

For many visitors, the most famous draw is the ancient university town of St Andrews, placed invitingly on their doorstep. Passionate golfers the world over are drawn to the hallowed links to face the challenges of the world's most famous golf course. For golfers celebrating a great round, or for the less fortunate seeking solace after a wearying test too far, Geoffrey and Katherine are waiting at The Peat Inn to restore body and soul.

Today as a restaurant with rooms, they continue the uninterrupted tradition of great hospitality that has endured at The Peat Inn since the 1750s, when it was built as a coaching inn. Now it is a contemporary country restaurant, offering relaxed service and the best in modern cuisine, in what is surely one of the loveliest corners of Scotland.

Geoffrey Smeddle
THE PEAT INN

The modern cuisine, based on classical techniques, has earned numerous awards, including one Michelin star.

WARM SALAD OF GLAZED MALLARD BREAST, ROAST HEART, QUINCE & COBNUTS

SERVES 4

Gewürztraminer (France)
The perfumed richness of this wine highlights the spice glaze.

Ingredients

Mallard Breast

2 Mallard ducks (oven ready, legs removed)
10ml vegetable oil
salt and pepper
2 sprigs thyme
35g unsalted butter

Duck Hearts

4 duck hearts (seasoned with salt)
vegetable oil (to fry)

Glaze

1 tsp each (cloves, juniper, black peppercorns, fennel seeds, coriander seeds)
1 star anise
250ml clear runny honey
1-2 tsp sherry vinegar

Pickled Shallot

100ml sweet wine such as Monbazillac
1 banana shallot (peeled, cut in rings)

Quince

1 quince (peeled, cut into wedges, core removed)
½ lemon (juice of)
15g unsalted butter
1 sprig thyme

Garnish

small parsley shoots
8 cobnuts or hazelnuts (halved)

Method

For The Glaze

Place the spices in a dry frying pan and toast over a gentle heat for a minute, or until they become aromatic, then remove at once to cool. Blitz to a coarse powder in a food processor. Transfer to a suitably sized container. Warm the honey and pour over the spices, mix the sherry vinegar in well and cover until needed. This will make more than is required for this recipe, but it is hard to make smaller quantities and it can be reserved for other uses. Stored at room temperature, it will last for 10 days.

For The Pickled Shallot

Soak the sliced shallot in the sweet wine until ready to serve.

For The Quince

Place the quince in a small pan and toss in the lemon juice, then add the thyme and the butter. Fry gently for 5 minutes, ensuring the slices of quince are laid flat. Turn each wedge over and repeat. Add the sweet wine, bring to a simmer and allow the fruit to poach as the liquid reduces. The quince should be tender and just cooked, but still holding its shape when the wine is reduced. If too firm, cover with foil and finish in the oven for a few minutes. Set aside to cool.

For The Mallard Breast

Preheat the oven to 180°C (fan).

Heat a large frying pan for 1 minute over a moderate to high heat, then add the vegetable oil. Season the duck crowns and seal all over until dark, golden brown. Add the butter and thyme, lay the duck on its side, then place in the oven for 6-8 minutes. Turn onto the opposite side and repeat. Remove from the oven and rest for 10 minutes, with the duck standing so the breast is downwards in the pan and the tail end is pointing upwards. Cut the breasts from the bone, trim them and lay them flesh-side down into the pan.

Chef's Tip

Don't discard the legs. We *confit* the leg meat as filling for ravioli or for use in canapés.

For The Duck Hearts

Heat a small pan over a high heat, add a little vegetable oil, then sear very briefly all over. Transfer them to the pan with the duck breasts.

To Serve

Spoon the glaze over the breasts and cut the breast in half, lengthways. Cut the hearts into two. Cut the slices of quince in half. Arrange 2 slices of breast meat, angled, on each plate and scatter the hearts and quince around. Arrange the pickled shallot on each breast. Garnish with herbs and cobnuts. Serve at once.

(see glossary)

ROAST WILD HALIBUT, POACHED ST ANDREWS BAY LOBSTER, BROCCOLI & BLOOD ORANGE

SERVES 4

A buttery Chardonnay, or a floral Viognier

Ingredients

Halibut

4 x 150g portions halibut (skinless, lightly seasoned with sea salt flakes)
10ml vegetable oil
butter (knob of)
lemon (wedge of)
1 rounded dsp chervil and tarragon (chopped)

Lobster

1 cooked St Andrews Bay lobster (tail and claws removed from the shell)
40g butter

Broccoli

2 heads broccoli
150ml cream (approximately)

Crosnes

20 crosnes (scrubbed clean)
chicken stock (to cover)

Garnish

1 blood orange (peeled, pith removed, segments diced)
fronds fennel herb

Chef's Tip

Tenderstem or purple sprouting broccoli are also lovely in this dish, or in late spring and summer you could use asparagus.

Method

For The Broccoli

Cut the heads off the broccoli and reserve 16 evenly sized, neat pieces to garnish. Also set aside 8 pieces of broccoli stem. Trim the stems to remove the outer layer of tough skin.

Chop the remaining florets into 2cm sized pieces and slice the stems into fine rounds. Cook the florets for 2 minutes in a large pan of well salted water, then chill at once in iced water, removing and drying them as soon as they are chilled. Repeat for the stems. Reserve the cooking water. Transfer to a blender and add a very small amount of the cooking water. Process to a smooth, thick purée, adding a dash more cooking water if needed. Finish with just enough cream to enrich the purée, but do not allow it to become too loose. Set aside.

For The Crosnes

Simmer the crosnes in the chicken stock until tender. Keep warm.

For The Halibut

Heat a wide non-stick pan over a high heat, add the oil and place the fillets fleshy-side down in the pan. Cook for 3-4 minutes, or until lightly browned. Add the butter, allowing it to froth up, then squeeze in the lemon juice. Spoon the juices in the pan over the fish. Carefully turn over, then baste well once more. Remove from the pan at once. The fish should still be a little underdone in the middle - the residual heat will finish cooking the flesh. Sprinkle over the chopped herbs, then spoon over the pan juices.

For The Lobster

Cut the lobster tail into 4 medallions and cut each claw in half, to give a piece of tail and claw per person. Heat a small frying pan, add a knob of butter and allow to foam. When lightly browned, add the lobster meat, frying very gently, spooning the butter over constantly. This will only require a couple of minutes to warm the meat.

To Serve

Heat the broccoli purée and taste for seasoning. Cook the florets and stems in salted water until *al dente*.

Swipe the purée on the plate, then set the fish to one side. Drain the lobster on absorbent paper and arrange on either side of the fish. Place the broccoli florets around the plate and scatter the orange, fennel herb and warm crosnes over the dish.
Serve immediately.

(see glossary)

RHUBARB & CUSTARD PANNA COTTA, VANILLA RICE PUDDING, RHUBARB SORBET

SERVES 4

Cadillac Dessert Wine (France)
A sweet but not overly sugary dessert wine, a neighbour to the more famous, and often sweeter, Sauternes. Because Cadillac is less famous, it is less expensive, offering outstanding value for a wine just as special as the more celebrated Sauternes.

Ingredients

Panna Cotta

240ml double cream
150g full-fat milk
1 vanilla pod
50g sugar
2 gelatine leaves (soaked in iced water)
1 lemon (zest of, optional)

Rhubarb Compôte

4 sticks forced rhubarb (trimmed, leaves removed)
few dashes Angostura bitters
8 dsp caster sugar

Vanilla Rice Pudding

60g unsalted butter
200g Carnaroli risotto rice
240ml full-fat milk
240ml double cream
1 vanilla pod (seeds of)
dash good quality vanilla essence
100g caster sugar (or to taste)
1 dsp crème fraîche

To Serve

pistachios (chopped)
rhubarb sorbet

4 glasses

Method

For The Panna Cotta

Heat the milk, cream and vanilla together with the sugar, then remove from the heat. Whisk in the softened gelatine and allow to cool slightly. Taste and adjust the sweetness as desired. You can also add a little lemon zest if you wish. Divide between the 4 glasses. Refrigerate to set for 2 hours.

For The Rhubarb Compôte

Preheat the oven to 180°C (fan).

Place the rhubarb in an ovenproof tray. Sprinkle the Angostura bitters over the stems of rhubarb, then sprinkle sugar over each stick. Add a few drops of water to the base of the pan. Bake for 30 minutes until tender, but still just holding its shape, then remove and chill. Once cold, chop the rhubarb finely and mix in any cooking juices from the tray. Taste for sweetness and set aside.

For The Vanilla Rice Pudding

Heat a wide saucepan over a very gentle heat for 1 minute, add the butter and allow to melt, but do not let it colour. Add the rice and cook gently, stirring all the time with a spatula for 8-10 minutes so the rice becomes translucent, but it must not colour.

Stir in the milk, cream and vanilla. Continue to simmer, stirring until the liquid is absorbed and the rice is tender.

If the liquid is absorbed, but the rice is still too starchy, add more milk and continue to cook until the rice is tender. Stir in the sugar, tasting as you go, then spread the rice pudding out on a tray to cool. Before serving, place in a bowl and stir in the crème fraîche. If it is very thick, add a little more cream or milk.

To Serve

Spread a layer of the rhubarb compôte across the surface of each panna cotta, then spoon some of the rice pudding across the compôte. Scatter over some chopped pistachios and place a scoop of rhubarb sorbet in the middle. Serve at once.

Chef's Tip

In high summer I like to replace the rhubarb and pistachios with either roasted or chopped, fresh strawberries and crumbled amaretti biscuits. In winter, plums or brambles work well.

220
PURSLANE RESTAURANT

33a St Stephen Street, Edinburgh, EH3 5AH

0131 226 3500
www.purslanerestaurant.co.uk Twitter: Purslane_1

idden in the stunning area of Stockbridge in Edinburgh, Purslane is the epitome of rustic, casual fine dining. The restaurant has a relaxed feel with no dress code or formality, allowing customers to feel at ease at all times.

Since opening in 2011, Purslane has showcased local produce with a mix of old and new techniques using worldwide influences.

It offers affordable dishes with a modern twist, a reasonably priced wine list and unobtrusive service. Chef/proprietor Paul Gunning heads up the team of chefs and friendly, front of house staff in this cosy restaurant. Paul forged his career working in some of the most reputable AA Rosette and Michelin starred establishments across the country, learning from chefs such as Marco Pierre White (River Room MPW) and Jeff Bland (Balmoral, Number One).

Paul doesn't take all the credit for Purslane's success. "The team, who have all worked here for over two and a half years, have helped evolve the restaurant into what it is today." Their hard work has helped them get into the Good Food Guide and retain their position for a second year, as well as being nominated for numerous awards as 'best fine dining restaurant'. The most recent award was during 'Stockfest' in Stockbridge where they won 'most innovative dish'.

"We feel strongly about the seasonality of the ingredients that are used, to ensure the best quality," says Paul. "We have tried to source most of our suppliers in the local area and around 80% are based in and around Stockbridge. We hope this will bring a sense of community to the restaurant and also help fellow small businesses."

Menus change regularly to accommodate the quality supply of seasonal produce that arrives at Purslane's door. Diners may choose from the fixed price à la carte menu or seven course tasting menu with matching wines.

Dining at Purslane offers all the elements of a great meal without the fuss, leaving guests to enjoy each other's company over a delicious meal and glass of wine.

SEARED SCALLOPS WITH GINGERBREAD, CARROT PUREE, ORANGE & ESCABECHE GARNISH

SERVES 4

Sauvignon Blanc Semillon, Suckfizzle, 2009 (Western Australia)

Ingredients

8 scallops (sliced in half)

Gingerbread

350g plain flour
1½ tsp bicarbonate of soda
1½ tsp ground cinnamon
4 tsp ground ginger
salt (pinch of)
110g butter
150g light brown sugar
3 tbsp golden syrup
3 tbsp black treacle
3 medium eggs (beaten)
7 tbsp milk

Carrot Purée

5 carrots
50g butter
50ml vegetable stock
100ml double cream
salt (pinch of)

Escabeche

1 carrot (finely sliced)
2 shallots (finely sliced)
salt (pinch of)
1 clove garlic
1 sprig tarragon
50ml white wine vinegar
25ml water

Garnish

1 orange (segmented)
micro herbs

2 loaf tins (lined or buttered)

Method

For The Gingerbread

Preheat the oven to 180°C.

Sift the flour, bicarbonate of soda, ground ginger, ground cinnamon and salt into a bowl. Gently heat the butter, sugar, syrup and treacle until the sugar has dissolved and the butter has just melted. Cool slightly, add the milk and beaten eggs, then add to the flour mixture. Beat until smooth, then divide into the prepared tins and bake for 50-60 minutes until they have risen and are just firm to touch. This recipe will make more than you need, but it freezes well, or can be enjoyed with your afternoon cuppa!

For The Carrot Purée

Finely slice the carrots and add to a pan with the butter, salt, cream and stock. Cover with a lid and cook on a medium heat until the carrots are cooked. Blitz until smooth.

For The Escabeche

Sweat the carrot and shallots in a little oil, with salt, garlic and the tarragon in a pan for 2 minutes, then add the vinegar and water. Cook for 3-5 minutes until the carrots just have a little crunch, then leave to cool in the pickling liquor.

To Serve

Sear the scallops in a hot pan with a little oil until golden on one side. Turn them over and finish by cooking for 20 seconds. Spread the carrot purée on the plate, place the scallops on the purée and garnish with the orange segments, escabeche, gingerbread and some micro herbs.

Chef's Tip

Use a really hot, non-stick pan for the scallops and don't turn them over until they are nicely caramelised. Once they are almost cooked, take them out the pan and the residual heat will cook them through.

ROAST RUMP OF BEEF, BEEF & POTATO TERRINE, CARAMELISED ONIONS, CELERIAC PUREE, KALE & WATERCRESS

SERVES 4

Carmenere, Armador, 2012 (Chile)

Ingredients

4 x 180g beef rumps

Celeriac Purée

1 celeriac (diced)
50g unsalted butter
50ml vegetable stock
100ml double cream
salt (pinch of)

Beef And Potato Terrine

2 ox cheeks (diced)
1 carrot (roughly chopped)
1 stick celery (roughly chopped)
1 small leek (roughly chopped)
3 sprigs thyme
2 cloves garlic
200ml red wine
sugar (pinch of)
salt (pinch of)
100ml beef stock
2 baking potatoes

Caramelised Onions

4 large onions (finely sliced)
oil (for frying)
salt (good pinch of)

To Serve

100g kale
1 bunch watercress (picked)

terrine mould

Method

For The Celeriac Purée

Add all the ingredients to a pan, cover with a lid and cook on a medium heat until the celeriac is cooked. Blitz until smooth.

For The Beef And Potato Terrine (Prepare ahead)

Marinate the ox cheeks overnight with the carrot, leek, celery, garlic, thyme, red wine, sugar and salt.

Remove the ox cheeks from the marinade and sear in a hot pan. Add the vegetables from the marinade, then *deglaze* with the red wine. Cover with the beef stock and braise for 3-4 hours until the meat is tender. Remove the meat and pass the stock through a sieve, then reduce by three quarters. Add back to the meat and mix until well incorporated, correct the seasoning, then put aside. Thinly slice the potatoes and *blanch* in boiling salted water. Remove and cool slightly on a wire rack. Line a terrine mould with cling film and arrange a layer of potatoes, then add a layer of ox cheek. Repeat this process 3 times. Cover and press in the fridge for at least 4 hours.

Chef's Tip

For the best results when making the terrine, try and press it overnight. You can also make ox cheek croquettes if there is any mixture left over from the terrine.

For The Caramelised Onions

Add the finely sliced onions to a hot pan with a little oil. Season with a good pinch of salt and cook slowly until the onions become soft and dark brown.

To Serve

Preheat the oven to 180°C.

Sear the beef rumps until golden brown, then finish in the oven for 8-10 minutes. Slice the terrine and warm through in the oven for 5 minutes. Cook the kale in boiling, salted water for 1 minute. Assemble on the plate and garnish with picked watercress.

(see glossary)

DARK CHOCOLATE MOUSSE, CRUMBLE & SALTED CARAMEL ICE CREAM

SERVES 4

Pedro Ximenez, Gutierrez Colosia (Spain)

Ingredients

Salted Caramel Ice Cream

150g caster sugar
salt (pinch of)
300ml full-fat milk
200ml double cream
1 tin condensed milk
1 tbsp glucose

Dark Chocolate Mousse

100g dark chocolate
4 medium eggs
50ml water
100g caster sugar
100ml double cream

Chocolate Ganache

150g 64% dark chocolate
25g unsalted butter
150ml double cream
Tia Maria (splash of)

Crumble

70g butter (soft)
20g cocoa powder
70g plain flour
65g caster sugar
salt (pinch of)

To Serve

tempered chocolate dome (optional - filled with some of the chocolate mousse)
salted caramel
almonds (chopped)
micro herbs

Method

For The Salted Caramel Ice Cream (Prepare ahead)

Caramelise the caster sugar, then add a pinch of salt. Add the milk, cream, condensed milk and glucose and warm until the salted caramel has dissolved into the rest of the mix. Chill, then churn and keep in the freezer until required.

For The Dark Chocolate Mousse

Break the chocolate into pieces, place in a bowl and gently melt over a pan of warm water (*bain-marie*).

Separate the egg whites and yolks into 2 separate bowls. Bring the water and caster sugar to 115°C.

Add half of the sugar mix to the egg whites and whisk to form a meringue. Add the other half to the egg yolks and whisk until cool. The egg yolks should be light, thick and creamy, roughly 4 times in volume.

Whisk the cream to a soft peak consistency. Let the chocolate cool slightly, then fold into the egg yolk mixture. Add the cream and meringue, gently folding in all the ingredients until they are well incorporated.

Chef's Tip

Don't overwork the mousse or the air will escape from it.

For The Chocolate Ganache

Melt the chocolate in a *bain-marie* with the butter. When melted, add the cream and mix until fully incorporated. Stir in the Tia Maria (or liqueur of your choice). Set in silicon moulds or in a container in the fridge. Cut to desired shape to serve.

For The Crumble

Preheat the oven to 180°C.

Rub the ingredients together to a crumb consistency. Pour onto a baking tray and bake for 12-15 minutes. Once cool, blitz to make a crumble.

To Serve

Fill the chocolate dome (if using) with some of the mousse. *Quenelle* some more mousse and a scoop of ice cream and set on top of the chocolate crumble along with the ganache. Dot with salted caramel, sprinkle with the almonds and garnish with micro herbs.

(see glossary)

230
RESTAURANT MARK GREENAWAY

69 North Castle Street, Edinburgh, EH2 3LJ

0131 226 1155
www.markgreenaway.com Twitter: @markgreenaway

There is nowhere that Mark Greenaway would rather be than in front of the stove at his North Castle Street restaurant, which is where he can be found during every service each week. You wouldn't think that this is the case with the level of exposure the restaurant receives both on Great British Menu and Channel 4's Sunday Brunch but this is just testament to how hard the whole team works, including Mark on his days off. His eponymous restaurant currently holds 3 AA Rosettes for culinary excellence and after just over a year of opening, was named one of the top 100 restaurants in the UK by both Restaurant Magazine and Square Meal.

Restaurant Mark Greenaway is both elegant and exciting - one of those rare dining rooms that manages to induce a sense of calm whilst encouraging anticipation. The journey to get to this point reflects over 22 years of learning and developing that has taken Mark Greenaway from the Highlands of Scotland to the shores of Australia and back again. Each dish is produced with seasonality and provenance as the guiding principle.

Mark believes that every great plate of food starts with the raw ingredients and therefore he works very closely with all of his suppliers, no matter how big or small, on an almost daily basis.

2015 has seen the exciting addition of a private dining room at Restaurant Mark Greenaway. The Balvenie Room is a private dining space like no other. The Georgian setting offers historic features; an exposed stone wall and the building's original stone stove. The intimate space, which can seat up to 16 guests, has been finished using unique art installations to complement 69 North Castle Street's structure.

Mark Greenaway photography: Paul Johnston www.coppermango.com

Acknowledged for its innovative dishes and admirable service, Restaurant Mark Greenaway is the proud holder of 3 AA Rosettes for culinary excellence, and has been named one of the top 100 restaurants in the UK by Restaurant Magazine and Square Meal.

SMOKED SALMON CANNELLONI WITH SAUCE GRIBICHE

SERVES 4

 Grüner Veltliner, 2013, Machherndl, Wachau (Austria)

Ingredients

Smoked Salmon Cannelloni

6 strips smoked salmon (very thinly sliced)
200g smoked salmon trimmings
100g crème fraîche
50ml double cream
2 tsp chives (chopped)

Sauce Gribiche

4 hard-boiled eggs (yolks discarded, whites finely diced)
100ml olive oil
½ bunch fresh chervil (chopped)
½ bunch fresh tarragon (chopped)
½ bunch fresh flat leaf parsley (finely shredded)
100g baby capers (drained)
100g cornichons (baby gherkins) (drained, finely diced)

Garnish (optional)

caviar
saffron mayonnaise

cookie cutter

Method

For The Smoked Salmon Cannelloni

Blend the smoked salmon trimmings together with the crème fraîche and cream until it forms a smooth mousse-like texture. Place in a small bowl, suitable to fit in your fridge, and fold through the chives and a little pinch of salt. Refrigerate for approximately 1 hour. Place the mousse mixture into a piping bag with a plain nozzle.

Lay out the remaining smoked salmon on cling film to form a large strip. Pipe the smoked salmon mousse along the length of the smoked salmon and roll up tightly together to form a cylinder. Twist the ends tightly and refrigerate for another hour. Cut the cylinder into 4 and remove the cling film.

Chef's Tip

If you don't fancy slicing the salmon yourself, get your local fishmonger to do it for you.

For The Sauce Gribiche

Mix all the ingredients in a bowl and gently fold together. Season with a little salt, but be careful as the capers can already be a little salty.

To Serve

Using a cookie cutter, press the gribiche around the inside to form a circle on the plate. Remove the cookie cutter and place the smoked salmon 'cannelloni' in the middle of the circle. In the restaurant, we garnish with a little caviar and saffron mayonnaise. This is, of course, an optional but delicious addition!

ROASTED PARTRIDGE, SPELT RISOTTO, DAMSON JUS

SERVES 4

'Are You Game?' Pinot Noir, 2012, Fowles Wine, Victoria (Australia)

Ingredients

Spelt Risotto

200g spelt
1 litre good quality chicken stock
2 banana shallots (peeled, finely diced)
1 clove garlic (crushed)
25g butter

Partridge

4 partridges (innards and feet removed)
40g butter
oil (enough to fry the birds)
3 sprigs thyme
2 cloves garlic (skin on, crushed)

Damson Jus

250g damsons (halved, stones removed)
800ml good quality chicken stock
300ml red wine
trimmings from the partridge

Method

For The Spelt Risotto

Sweat the shallot and garlic in the butter until it becomes translucent and soft. Add the spelt and cook in the butter for about 3 minutes. Pour in all of the chicken stock, turn down the heat and simmer for 2 hours until the spelt becomes swollen and has absorbed all of the liquid.

For The Partridge

Preheat the oven to 185°C (fan).

Melt the butter in the oil in a pan and add the partridges. Season generously with salt and brown the birds all over before transferring the pan to the oven. Cook for 8-10 minutes. Take the pan from the oven and add the thyme and garlic. Baste the buttery garlic and thyme mixture over the bird, making sure you coat each side and it is evenly covered. Rest the bird for 8-10 minutes.

Carve the partridge as you would a chicken, removing the breasts and legs from the bones. Cover the meat with foil and set aside while you make the jus.

For The Damson Jus

Reduce the red wine and add any partridge trimmings. Add the chicken stock and reduce by half. Strain the partridge out otherwise the sauce will become too 'gamey'. Continue to reduce the sauce until it coats the back of a spoon, or is the consistency of single cream. Stir in the damsons.

Please note: At the restaurant I serve this dish with chervil root purée, cep croutons and burnt cream. I wrap the partridge legs in pancetta and cook them separately from the crown. This is an optional step but worthwhile trying at home if you have the time.

Chef's Tip

This recipe is one for the partridge season which runs from September to February in Scotland. Ask your butcher to fully prepare the partridges for you.

RHUBARB TRIFLE

SERVES 4

Château Laville, 2009, Sauternes (France)

Ingredients

Shortbread Granola With Pistachios

200g butter
100g caster sugar
100g pistachios (shelled)
300g plain flour

Poached Rhubarb With Hibiscus

2 sticks rhubarb
100ml water
100g caster sugar
5g dried hibiscus flowers

Rhubarb Crisps

300g rhubarb purée
100g icing sugar
½ lime (juice of)

Rhubarb Meringue

2 egg whites
150g caster sugar
rhubarb crisps (a few of)

Crème Brûlée Mix

500ml double cream
7 egg yolks
120g caster sugar
2 vanilla pods

Rhubarb Compôte

150g rhubarb (small dice)
100g caster sugar
50ml water
1 vanilla pod (seeds of)

4 glasses

Chef's Tip

This recipe is adaptable. You can use whatever fruit is in season. It works equally well with summer berries.

Method

For The Shortbread Granola With Pistachios

Cream the butter and sugar together, then mix in the pistachios and the flour. Roll the mixture into logs, wrap in cling film and place in the freezer until frozen, for about 1 hour.

Preheat the oven to 180°C (fan).

Unwrap the logs and grate them onto a silicon mat or lined baking tray. Bake until golden brown, for about 9-10 minutes. Break up with a fork and leave to cool.

For The Poached Rhubarb With Hibiscus

Cut the rhubarb into 5cm batons. Boil the water, sugar and hibiscus together until the sugar melts. Put the rhubarb and syrup into a vacuum pack bag (on high) and cook in a water bath at 64°C for 1 hour. Alternatively poach in gently simmering water.

For The Rhubarb Crisps (Prepare ahead)

Blend together all of the ingredients and pass through a *chinois* onto a silicon mat or lined baking tray.

Spread to an even thickness and dehydrate at the highest setting on your dehydrator for 12 hours. After 12 hours, turn out on to a chopping board and cut into equilateral triangles or desired shape. Dehydrate for a further 8 hours. Alternatively, dry in the oven at 80°C (fan off).

For The Rhubarb Meringue

Place the egg whites and sugar into a medium-sized metal bowl and place over a *bain-marie*. Stir the egg whites and sugar until the sugar has completely dissolved. Remove from the heat.

Place the egg white mixture into a mixer and whisk, on full, for 8 minutes or until slightly cooled.

Spoon into a piping bag and pipe the meringues onto a lined baking tray.

Blitz a few of the rhubarb crisps in a spice blender and sprinkle the powder over the meringues. Bake in the oven at 130°C (fan) for 15 minutes.

For The Crème Brûlée Mix

Scrape seeds out of the vanilla pods and add to the eggs yolks and sugar, whisk thoroughly. Bring the cream and vanilla pod to a simmer. Pour the cream through a *chinois* straight onto the yolk mixture. Put the mixture in a clean pan and place back on the heat. Cook out to 82°C using a thermometer. Pass through a *chinois* onto a tray and chill until set, for about 4 hours.

Once set, decant into a bowl and whisk to break down the crème brûlée. Spoon into a piping bag and chill until required.

For The Rhubarb Compôte

Using the sugar make a dry caramel in a non-stick pan. *Deglaze* with the water and vanilla seeds, then immediately pour over the diced rhubarb. Cling film well and chill until required.

To Serve

Serve in glasses as pictured.

(see glossary)

MICHELIN STAR SPOTLIGHT...

GEOFFREY SMEDDLE

CHEF PATRON, THE PEAT INN

I started my career working with Herbert Berger at The Café Royal and for Christopher Galvin in London. I then moved up to Glasgow to open Terence Conran's Etain. I've worked in numerous locations around the world, including a stint at the renowned Four Seasons Hotel in Chicago, however I had the opportunity to take over The Peat Inn in Fife in 2006 and I knew it would be a challenge I didn't want to miss out on.

The enduring appeals of Fife for me as a chef are the exquisite products surrounding us. Scotland, of course, is renowned for its world class produce. I often feel that our Fife coastline and countryside offer a distilled version in miniature of all that is great about Scotland: wild herbs, game, shellfish, fruits, berries and vegetables travel to the kitchen from the rich countryside immediately surrounding us. Asparagus, for instance, can be picked for us on the morning that we order it and delivered in time for lunch. Lamb comes from a local estate overlooking the sea and our rare breed pork is found just a few miles from us, as the crow (or wild pigeon) flies. A wonderful collection of restaurants and hotels makes Fife a truly exciting destination for the discerning visitor. Discovering the growing movement of local craft beer brewers, as well as the gin and whisky distillers, completes a vibrant food and drink scene.

I could not imagine a more delightful location from which to run my restaurant. Visit Fife and you will be sure to fall in love with our truly special area.

St Andrews, Fife, KY15 5LH.
01334 840 206 www.thepeatinn.co.uk

242 RISTORANTE LA PARMIGIANA

447 Great Western Road, Glasgow, G12 8HH

0141 334 0686
www.laparmigiana.co.uk Twitter: @LaParmigianaGla

Situated in Glasgow's busy West End at Kelvinbridge, the elegant restaurant transports you from the hustle and bustle of the big city, to a cosy and relaxed atmosphere, strengthened further by the restaurant's white table cloths and pristine, highly trained waiters.

La Parmigiana was founded by the Giovanazzi family in 1978 and is now in its third generation of the same family. Currently run by Sandro and son Matteo Giovanazzi, with head chef Peppino Camilli, La Parmigiana is known for being one of the foremost Italian restaurants in the country and prides itself in using the finest, fresh ingredients sourced from local producers.

La Parmigiana has a long and proud tradition of serving the very finest Italian food and its popularity amongst Glasgow's Italian community is testimony to the authenticity and quality of the cuisine, and the exceptional Italian wine cellar attracts new customers daily, and keeps them coming back for more.

The restaurant's menus, which are changed frequently, are made up of traditional northern Italian dishes and showcase the diversity of skills of the chefs, whilst also incorporating a wonderful showcase of the rich Scottish larder.

AMPARI

Ristorante La Parmigiana has a long and proud history of Italian cuisine.

LOBSTER RAVIOLI IN CREAM & BASIL SAUCE

SERVES 4

Carpene Malvolti Prosecco Superiore (Italy)

Ingredients

Pasta

200g 00 flour
2 eggs
1 tbsp extra virgin olive oil

For The Lobster Stuffing

1 whole lobster
½ onion (finely chopped)
1 medium potato (boiled in its skin)
5 tbsp Parmigiano Reggiano (grated)
1 whole egg
butter (large knob of)
salt and black pepper

Cream And Basil Sauce

250ml double cream
2 tsp tomato purée
fresh basil (small bunch of)

Garnish

basil leaves
Parmigiano Reggiano (grated)

Method

For The Pasta Dough

Pile up the flour on a flat table and make a well in the middle to pour the egg mixture into. Beat together the eggs and oil, then pour into the well. Slowly mix in the flour from around the walls of the well until you have a more solid dough. Once the dough does not run, knead the rest of the flour into the mixture and allow to rest for 15 minutes.

For The Lobster Stuffing

Drop the whole lobster into a pot of salted, boiling water and cook for 10 minutes, then drain and leave to cool. Remove all the meat from the shells including the claws and chop finely. Fry the onion in a pan with the butter until transparent, then stir in the chopped lobster meat. Remove the skin from the potato and mash so that there are no lumps, then mix with the lobster and onion - this will help to bind the filling. Allow to cool. Once cooled, add the Parmigiano and egg and mix well. Season to taste.

Chef's Tip

Use all the lobster meat as it is expensive. The shell can be used for a lobster stock.

To Make The Ravioli (Makes 16)

Divide the pasta dough in 2 and roll each half to the same shape so that one can sit on top of the other once the stuffing has been added. Roll to a thickness of just under 2mm. Put enough stuffing for each parcel, with plenty of room between the stuffing, on one half of the dough and lay the other half of the dough over so that it covers all the stuffing. Then, pushing out as much air as possible, push down hard on the edges of the ravioli so that the pasta seals. Once each parcel has been sealed, cut with a ravioli cutter. These can be any shape you want them to be. Sprinkle lightly with flour and set aside.

For The Cream And Basil Sauce

Tear up some basil leaves and place in a frying pan with the cream. Bring to the boil. Once bubbling, add the tomato purée and mix well.

To Serve

Bring a large pot of salted water to the boil. Drop the ravioli into the boiling water and remove when they float, about 2 minutes. Drain and add them to the pasta sauce. Cook the ravioli in the sauce until it thickens slightly.

Plate 4 ravioli per person with enough sauce to cover. Garnish with basil leaves and freshly grated Parmigiano.

ZUPPA DI PESCE (ITALIAN FISH STEW)

SERVES 4

Vermentino Bolgheri Tenuta Guado Al Tasso (Italy)

Ingredients

Zuppa Di Pesce

1½ onions
1 clove
2 bay leaves
2 carrots
3 celery sticks (1 finely chopped)
1 tomato (finely chopped)
½ medium heat chilli
½ green pepper (seeded, cut in slices)
150ml dry white wine
flat leaf parsley (small bunch of)
400g mussels (scrubbed, beards removed)
300g clams (soaked overnight to remove any sand)
200g gurnard (cleaned)
8 medium prawns (heads on)
1 squid tube (finely sliced)
salt and black pepper

To Serve

bread (toasted)

Method

For The Zuppa Di Pesce

Stud 1 onion with the clove and 1 of the bay leaves and put in a pan with 2½ litres of water, along with the carrots, 2 sticks of celery, half of the bunch of parsley and any fish trimmings (lobster shells or prawn shells would also be ideal). Bring to the boil, then lower the heat and allow to simmer for 30 minutes to make a court-bouillon. Strain and keep hot.

Finely chop the remaining half onion and fry, with some extra virgin olive oil, in a frying pan with the finely chopped celery, tomato, the green pepper and the chilli until they are all softened. Season the fish and add to the frying pan followed by the white wine. Cover and cook for 5 minutes. When the white wine has reduced by half, cover the contents with the hot *court-bouillon* and add the other bay leaf. Allow to cook for a further 10 minutes until all the fish is properly cooked.

Break some fresh parsley over the top of the stew and serve with some hearty, toasted bread.

Chef's Tip

You can use whatever sea fish or crustacean is available in the fishmongers.

(see glossary)

AMARETTO TIRAMISU

SERVES 4

 *Passito di Pantelleria (Italy)*

Ingredients

400g Savoiardi biscuits (lady fingers)

Mascarpone Cream

250g mascarpone cheese
2 egg whites
2 egg yolks
100g caster sugar
200ml double cream
100ml Amaretto

Coffee Mixture

1 litre strong coffee
100g caster sugar
200ml Marsala

Cappuccino Ice Cream

200ml full-fat milk
1 vanilla pod (scraped)
2 eggs
150g caster sugar
175ml strong coffee (cooled)
200ml double cream

Garnish

cocoa powder (for dusting)
Amaretti biscuits (crumbled)
tempered chocolate cup (optional)
raspberries

Method

For The Mascarpone Cream

Whisk the egg whites in a bowl until they form stiff peaks.

Beat the egg yolks and the sugar in a separate bowl until pale and fluffy. Add the double cream and Amaretto to the yolk mix, then gently fold in the mascarpone. Finally, fold in the egg whites.

For The Coffee Mixture

Mix the ingredients together until all the sugar has melted, leave to cool until tepid.

To Assemble The Tiramisu

Pour one third of the mascarpone cream into a high sided serving dish. Then, one by one, dip the Savoiardi biscuits into the coffee mixture for around 4 seconds each, until just softening, then lay a full layer over the mascarpone cream. Cover with another third of the mascarpone cream and repeat with the Savoiardi for the next layer. Cover with the last of the mascarpone cream and place in the fridge overnight to set.

For The Cappuccino Ice Cream

Pour the milk into a pan with the seeds of the vanilla pod and bring to the boil. Remove from the heat and leave to cool. Beat the eggs with the sugar in a bowl until pale, then add the coffee, followed by the cream and the milk. Mix well, then pour into an ice cream machine and churn until almost firm. Store in the freezer.

To Serve

Dust the tiramisu with cocoa powder and serve with the cappuccino ice cream in a tempered chocolate cup. Decorate the plate with crushed Amaretti biscuits and raspberries.

Chef's Tip

I have always liked a tiramisu with a good kick of alcohol but it's all down to personal taste how much you put in. Make the tiramisu the day before to allow it to set and the flavours to develop.

252 ROAD HOLE RESTAURANT

Old Course Hotel, Golf Resort & Spa, St Andrews, Fife, KY16 9SP

01334 474 371
www.oldcoursehotel.co.uk Twitter: @oldcoursehotel

The 3 AA Rosette awarded Road Hole Restaurant commands an unrivalled position high on the hotel's fourth floor with spectacular views across the Old Course, including the Road Hole and iconic Swilcan Bridge.

The restaurant, one of no fewer than five unique dining experiences at the resort, is the 'home of Scottish cuisine in the home of golf'. The team of highly talented chefs, led by executive chef Martin Hollis, draws on inspiration from its location, working closely with producers and suppliers to use the very best of Scotland's larder, providing exceptional, seasonal, dining experiences. Gordon Shaw, restaurant manager, and his team offer guests the very best of 5 star customer service.

Current dishes include an 'East Neuk lobster gratin with parsley purée and an Arran mustard hollandaise' starter, a main of 'venison loin with suet pudding, red cabbage choucroute, shallot purée, confit celeriac with kale' and 'heather honey parfait with rhubarb sorbet and ginger crumble' dessert.

On the same floor is the iconic Road Hole Bar, boasting more than 250 whiskies, unique cocktails, as well as the Road Hole Deck, high above the Road Hole tee with views that take in the Old, New, Jubilee and Eden Courses.

The Road Hole Restaurant, open for lunches Friday to Sunday and for dinner Wednesday to Sunday, is a 'must visit' for foodies and for wine lovers. Our sommelier, Remi Fischer, is proud to talk guests through the restaurant's AA awarded Notable Wine List.

The location, combined with the bar and open air deck, provide a never-to-be-forgotten experience.

Executive chef, Martin Hollis, leads the Road Hole Restaurant's kitchen brigade, fronted by Craig McAllister. Together with their team, they retained the restaurant's 3 AA Rosettes in 2015 - an award held for 10 consecutive years.

FOIE GRAS A LA PLANCHA & BRULEE, CONFIT LEG CROUSTILLANT, MEDJOOL DATE, SOUR CHERRY

SERVES 4

Riesling Vieilles Vignes, Cave de Turckheim 2009 (France)

Ingredients

Foie Gras A La Plancha And Brûlée

1 lobe Perigord foie gras
100ml white port, 50ml brandy, 50ml Madeira
ground coriander (pinch of)
mixed spice (pinch of), sel rose (pinch of)
190ml double cream
2 medium eggs, 20g brown sugar

Confit Leg Croustillant

2 duck legs (skin scored)
herb rub (50g pink salt, 50g Maldon salt,
3 star anise, 10g coriander seeds,
4 cardamom pods (crushed)
1 litre duck fat
4 sprigs thyme, ½ orange (zest of)
3 bay leaves
4 sheets filo pastry, clarified butter (to brush)

Medjool Date Purée

100ml brandy, 1 sprig thyme, 1 bay leaf
250g Medjool dates (deseeded)
100ml water

Sour Cherry Chutney

300g shallots (finely diced)
½ cinnamon stick
5 cardamom pods (toasted, crushed)
1 clove garlic, 2 sprigs thyme, 2 bay leaves
50ml cider vinegar
250g brown sugar
1kg cherries (deseeded)
50g Granny Smith apple (peeled, ½ cm diced)

Garnish

pistachios (chopped)
nasturtium leaves and edible flowers

4 rings (lined with cling film)

Method

For The Fois Gras A La Plancha And Brûlée

Cut 4 portions from the foie gras and set aside. Dice 170g of the remaining foie gras. Reduce the alcohol to a syrup in a pan. Add the salt, spices and cream. Heat to 60°C, pass through a fine sieve. Blend in the diced foie gras and eggs. Pour into prepared rings, steam at 85°C for 10-15 minutes.

Chef's Tip

Remove the foie gras from the fridge 10 minutes before you plan on cooking it to ensure faster, more even cooking.

For The Confit Leg Croustillant (Prepare ahead)

Marinate the legs in the rub for 12 hours in the fridge. Wash the legs thoroughly and *confit* in the duck fat at 140°C for approximately 1½-2½ hours. Allow the legs to cool to room temperature in the fat. Remove the hardened fat and pick the meat off the legs. Mix the leg meat with the thyme and orange zest. Vacuum pack in a small bag and press flat to 2cm thickness, place in the fridge until it is set. Alternatively, wrap tightly in cling film and press. Remove the bag or cling film and brush the top of the meat with clarified butter. Place 1 sheet of filo on top and smooth it out. Brush the filo with clarified butter and place on the second layer of filo, again smoothing it out. Turn the meat over and repeat the process on the other side. Cut the filo parcels into lengths of 6cm x 2cm.

For The Medjool Date Purée

Flambé the brandy, add the herbs and reduce to a syrup. Remove the herbs and add the dates and water. Simmer until the dates have broken down and the liquid becomes thick. Purée until smooth and pass through a fine sieve.

For The Sour Cherry Chutney

Sweat the shallots, spices and herbs in a pan with a little oil, without colouring. Add in the vinegar and cook out. Stir in the sugar and cherries and simmer until thick. Add the apple and cook to the desired consistency.

To Assemble The Dish

Plate the foie gras, remove the rings and sprinkle with sugar. Caramelise with a blow torch. Griddle the *confit* duck until the filo is crisp and the meat hot. Sear 4 portions of foie gras until cooked. Assemble with the other elements as per the picture.

(see glossary)

MONKFISH, PERSILLADE NOISETTE, LANGOUSTINE, MORTEAU SAUSAGE, PINK FIR APPLE POTATO, BURNT LEEK

SERVES 4

Etna Rosso, Tenuta Delle Terre Nere DOC 2012 (Italy)

Ingredients

Monkfish

4 x 125g monkfish portions
20g Shony seaweed
salt (pinch of), 200g caul fat
50g unsalted butter (to baste)

Persillade Noisette

150g parsley (finely chopped)
6g garlic (microplaned)
1 lemon (zest of, microplaned)
20g lilliput capers, 200g unsalted butter

Pink Fir Apple Potato Salad

500g Pink Fir apple potatoes (whole, unpeeled)
8g garlic, 5g bay leaves, 3g thyme leaves
2g lemon peel
3 oysters (shucked)
60g pasteurised egg yolk
50g crème fraîche, 100ml pomace oil
10g Avruga caviar, ½ lemon (spritz of)
10g dill (finely chopped)

Baby Leeks

8 baby leeks, 50ml rapeseed oil
4g thyme, 2g bay leaf

Lemon Purée

5 cardamom pods (crushed)
100g caster sugar, 100g lemon juice
2g thyme, 60g ultratex

Langoustines

8 large langoustines (*blanched*, refreshed, peeled)
250g kataifi pastry, 8 basil leaves

1 Morteau sausage (sautéed, diced)

Garnish

turnip tops

Method

For The Monkfish

Season the monkfish with the seaweed and salt, and wrap in the caul fat. Vacuum pack and set aside.

For The Persillade Noisette

Mix the parsley, zest, garlic and capers together. Heat the butter on a low heat and allow to separate. Season and whisk gradually until it turns to a nut brown colour. Stir in the other ingredients. Adjust the seasoning if required. Serve warm.

For The Pink Fir Apple Potato Salad

Boil the potatoes with the herbs, garlic and lemon peel until tender. Drain and allow to air dry. Peel whilst still warm and cut into 5cm dice.

Blend the oysters, egg and crème fraîche until smooth. Slowly add in the oil to thicken the mixture. Season with salt. Heat gently to serve and season with dill, caviar and lemon juice.

For The Baby Leeks

Trim the tops and roots of the leeks and wash thoroughly. Dress with the rapeseed oil and season. Vacuum pack with the herbs and steam until tender. Plunge the steamed leeks in iced water straight after. Char to serve.

For The Lemon Purée

Bring all the ingredients, except the ultratex, to the boil. Set aside and cool for 30 minutes. Blend in the ultratex until dissolved and the mixture has thickened.

For The Langoustine

Lay the pastry strips out flat. Season the langoustine and wrap a basil leaf around the centre. Lay on top of the outstretched pastry and roll as tightly as possible.

Chef's Tip

If you're struggling to wrap the kataifi pastry around the langoustine, try brushing on a little thinned egg white to soften and hold it whilst you work.

To Assemble The Dish

Sous vide the monkfish at 53°C for 15 minutes. When cooked, remove from the bag and dust lightly with plain flour. Seal all sides gently in a pan and baste with foaming butter. Set aside somewhere warm and allow to rest for 4 minutes.

Deep fry the langoustine until golden brown, trim off both ends and cut in half. Place all the elements on the plate and pipe on the lemon purée. Garnish with turnip tops and serve.

(see glossary)

MINT CREME, COMPRESSED STRAWBERRIES, BUTTER SHORTBREAD

SERVES 4

Laurent-Perrier 'Demi-sec' NV (France)

Ingredients

Mint Crème

100ml milk
60g caster sugar
2g mint leaves
400ml double cream
7g gelatine (softened)

Strawberry Leather

300g strawberry purée
30g caster sugar
2g agar agar

Butter Shortbread

100g butter
50g icing sugar
salt (pinch of)
½ lemon (zest of)
1 egg yolk
125g flour

Lime Gel

150ml lime juice
50g caster sugar
1g agar agar

Pâté De Brique Tuile

100g soft dark brown sugar
50g butter
50ml maple syrup
3 sheets pâté de brique

Compressed Strawberries

12 small strawberries (halved - may be served not compressed)

Garnish

crystallised mint fragments
strawberry purée (reserved from the strawberry leather)

Method

For The Mint Crème

Heat the milk and sugar then remove from the heat, add the mint leaves and blend. Heat up 100ml of cream to dissolve the gelatine. Mix all the ingredients together and pass through a fine sieve. Set in a tray lined with baking paper and place in fridge for 2-3 hours until completely set.

Chef's Tip

The mint crème is a very versatile recipe. Try changing out the mint for basil or ginger.

For The Strawberry Leather (Prepare ahead)

Boil all the ingredients for 1 minute, stirring constantly. Refrigerate in a container until cold, then blitz until smooth. Spread very thinly on a silicon mat (reserve some for plating). Dry overnight at 60°C. Store in an airtight container.

For The Butter Shortbread

Mix the butter, sugar, salt and lemon zest until combined. Mix in the egg yolk, followed by the flour. Bring the mixture together and roll into a sausage, cover with cling film and refrigerate. Once chilled, remove the cling film and slice ½cm thick discs. Place on a baking tray and bake at 160°C (fan) for 10 minutes.

For The Lime Gel

Boil all the ingredients in a small pan for 1 minute. Pour into a container and refrigerate until cold, then blitz until smooth. Store in a squeezy bottle.

For The Pâté De Brique Tuile

Brush the pastry sheets with the syrup and stack on top of each other. Bake between 2 baking trays at 180°C (fan) for 12-15 minutes.

For The Compressed Strawberries

Compress for 2 cycles (30 seconds) in a vac pack machine.

To Assemble

Cut the mint crème into fingers (1½ x 10cm) and plate on a swipe of purée. Dot the plate with lime gel. Break off pieces of shortbread and large pieces of tuile. Arrange all elements as shown and scatter with mint fragments.

262 ROCCA RESTAURANT

The Links, St Andrews, Fife, KY16 9JQ

01334 472 549
www.roccarestaurant.com Twitter: @roccastandrews

At Rocca St Andrews, the recipe for success is a fusion of exquisite food with a backdrop of one of the world's most famous sporting locations, the Old Course. Like the many champions who have graced the hallowed course, Rocca too tops the leaderboard as one of only 25 restaurants in the country with 3 AA Rosettes, a reward for the creativity and passion of the Rocca family.

The close team of passionate and skilled chefs has lifted Rocca to be one of the finest dining experiences on the beautiful east coast of Fife, from where they have an amazing larder of local produce to choose from. Rocca features Scottish cooking with a special Italian twist.

The front of house team is led by Sue who, with her talented team of young, bubbly and knowledgeable staff, will host your dining experience with energy and enthusiasm.

With a real pedigree in both the front-of-house and in the kitchen, you can rest assured a visit to Rocca with its understated glamour and outstanding food will live long in the memory.

Come and visit them and let their passion for food become your passion for delicious dining.

Executive head chef David Aspin has worked in many distinguished kitchens and is the driving force in the Rocca kitchen, nurturing new talent, creating new tastes and striving for perfection. Head chef Jamie Scott was crowned MasterChef: The Professionals 2014 champion, a huge achievement, of which the Rocca family is very proud.

ROASTED ARDNAMURCHAN SCALLOPS, BLOOD ORANGE, CHICORY & HAZELNUTS

SERVES 4

Insolia, Principi di Butera, Sicily (Italy)

Ingredients

Roasted Scallops

8 diver caught Ardnamurchan scallops (roe and skirt removed)
1 tsp curry powder
1 tsp fine sea salt
50g butter
½ orange (squeeze of)

Braised Chicory

2 white chicory
100ml freshly squeezed orange juice (plus zest of 3 oranges)
3g citric acid
20ml red wine vinegar
1 bouquet garni

Dressing

1 tsp wholegrain mustard
1 blood orange (juice of)
100ml white wine vinegar
1 tsp honey
50ml hazelnut oil

Garnish

50g hazelnuts (chopped)
2 blood oranges (segmented)
Iberico ham
blood orange purée
apple sticks
hazelnut oil

Method

For The Roasted Scallops

Combine the salt and curry powder. Season the scallops with the salt mixture and cook in a hot pan for 1 minute. Add the butter and turn the scallops over. Add a squeeze of orange juice, coat in the butter and remove from the pan. Reserve the juices.

For The Braised Chicory

Place all ingredients into a vacuum pack bag, seal on a high setting and steam for 27 minutes until tender. Cool, pat dry and trim. Alternatively, the chicory can be braised slowly.

Half the chicory lengthways and gently reheat in the reserved cooking liquor from the scallops.

For The Dressing

Mix the mustard, orange juice, honey and vinegar together, slowly adding the hazelnut oil until *emulsified*.

To Serve

Neatly place the scallops and chicory in the centre of the plate. Dress with the garnishes and mustard dressing and finish with a drizzle of hazelnut oil.

(see glossary)

PERTHSHIRE SADDLE OF HARE, CABBAGE, CIVET SAUCE

SERVES 4

 *Sasseo Primitivo Salento, Apulia (Italy)*

Ingredients

Saddle Of Hare

1 hare saddle (loins removed)
100g baby leaf spinach (picked, *blanched*)
12 slices Parma ham, salt and pepper

Red Cabbage

16 red cabbage leaves (cut into 4cm circles)
200ml red wine, 2 star anise
1 tsp coriander seeds, 1 tsp pink peppercorns
1 tbsp redcurrant jelly

Green Cabbage

16 Savoy cabbage leaves (cut into 4cm circles)
150ml chicken stock, 100g butter (diced)

Carrots

4 medium yellow carrots
200g sea salt, 200g flour
8 egg whites, 150ml chicken stock
100g butter (diced)

Civet Sauce

1 hare carcass (chopped up into small pieces)
4 shallots
8 button mushrooms
1 tsp coriander seeds, 2 star anise
1 tsp black peppercorns
4 cloves garlic
100ml red wine, 75ml brandy, 75ml port
100ml brown chicken stock

Red Cabbage Purée

1/4 red cabbage (finely sliced)
200ml red wine
200ml chicken stock
1 star anise, 2 bay leaves
50g redcurrant jelly

Garnish

pistachios (whole and ground)
salt baked beetroot, beetroot powder

Method

For The Saddle Of Hare

Lay a sheet of cling film flat on your surface. Layer the Parma ham on the cling film, overlapping the ham slightly, then place the *blanched* spinach on top. Place the hare in the centre and season. Roll the hare in the spinach and ham to form a tight sausage. Tie the ends tightly.

Bring a pan of water to the boil, turn off the heat and cool for 2-3 minutes. Add the hare and poach for 5 minutes. Remove from the water and rest for 2 minutes. Add a dash of olive oil to a non-stick pan, bring to a light 'smoke', then add the hare. Colour all over, add a knob of butter, allow to foam, then baste for 30 seconds. Remove and allow to rest for 5 minutes.

For The Red Cabbage

Place all the ingredients, except the cabbage circles, in a pan and bring to the boil. Add the red cabbage circles and cook until the liquid is syrupy.

For The Green Cabbage

Bring the chicken stock and butter to the boil and add the cabbage leaves. Cook for 1½ minutes, then remove and season.

For The Carrots

Preheat the oven to 160°C (fan).

Mix the flour and salt together, then add egg whites to make a firm dough. Wrap the carrots individually in the dough.
Bake for 20 minutes. Remove from the crust and cut into the desired shape.

For The Civet Sauce

Preheat the oven to 170°C (fan).

Divide the bones into 2 piles. Place half on an oiled baking tray and transfer to the oven for 15 minutes. Caramelise the other half in a heavy bottomed pan over a high heat. Add the vegetables and cook for 2 minutes. Stir in the aromats and cook for a further 2 minutes.

Add the alcohol and reduce. Pour in the stock, bring to the boil, then simmer for 10 minutes until thick and glossy. Add the baked bones and allow to sit for 5 minutes. Pass through a fine sieve.

For The Red Cabbage Purée

Place all ingredients in a heavy bottomed pan and bring to the boil. Simmer for 25 minutes. Strain the liquid, then blend. Pass through a fine sieve and season with salt.

To Assemble

Swipe the red cabbage purée on the plate. Cut the hare into quarters, set on the purée and adorn with the cabbage discs. Garnish as pictured.

(see glossary)

CHOCOLATE PAVE & COFFEE SYRUP

SERVES 4

Recioto Della Valpolicella, Veneto (Italy)

Ingredients

Cocoa Sponge

3 medium free-range eggs
75g caster sugar
50g cocoa powder

Mousse

50ml water
125g sugar
3 egg yolks
1 egg white
175g Valrhona 70% dark chocolate (melted)
250ml double cream

Chocolate Sauce

100g caster sugar
60ml water
35g cocoa powder
80ml double cream

Coffee Syrup

25g caster sugar
50ml espresso coffee
5g liquid glucose

Garnish

chocolate crumb
chocolate (grated)
edible flowers
chocolate tuile biscuits

1 rectangular, medium-sized, loose-bottomed cake tin (lightly greased)

Method

For The Cocoa Sponge

Preheat the oven to 150°C (fan).

Whisk the eggs and sugar together until pale and doubled in volume. Sieve and fold in the cocoa powder. Bake for 15 minutes in the prepared tin. Cool in the fridge for 15 minutes.

For The Mousse

Heat the sugar and water to 121°C. Whisk the egg yolks until pale and creamy. Add the sugar solution and whisk until cold. Whisk the egg whites to soft peaks. Fold together with the melted chocolate and the cooled egg mixture until well incorporated. Carefully spoon the mousse on top of the sponge and set in the fridge for 2 hours.

For The Chocolate Sauce

Boil the sugar, water and cocoa powder together. Add the cream, bring back to the boil, then cool completely.

For The Coffee Syrup

Heat the espresso, sugar and liquid glucose together.

To Serve

Cut the dessert into 5cm x 10cm rectangles. Carefully spread on some of the chocolate sauce, dot the coffee syrup on the side and garnish as pictured.

MICHELIN STAR SPOTLIGHT...
MICHAEL SMITH

As co-owner and director of The Three Chimneys, I have maintained its reputation and considerable critical acclaim by consistently creating and evolving dishes that reflect the restaurant's surroundings, specifically utilising as much of the superb Skye and Scottish natural larder as possible. My original take on traditional Scottish gastronomy, inspired by classical techniques, has received many accolades, including a top five placing in The New York Times food critic Franck Bruni's 'Favourite Destinations in the World', and most recently, in September 2014, being awarded a Michelin star.

Having first experienced commercial kitchens in my home city of Inverness, aged just 15, as a part time kitchen porter in a local restaurant, I quickly decided to pursue a career as a chef. This decision was reinforced in 1988 when I secured a place in the brigade of Arisaig House on the west coast of Scotland where I stayed for three years working under chef Matthew Burns. From there I moved to London, initially working at Le Gavroche before moving to Le Pont De La Tour and most significantly, spending four years as senior sous chef with Jeremy Lee at Blue Print Café. From there, I moved back to Scotland, commissioning three new Glasgow restaurants, firstly with Andrew Radford's Blue, then Arta and Gong with Stefan King's G1 Group, between 1999 and 2003.

As a passionate ambassador of Scottish gastronomy, I feel fortunate to be asked to participate in many events in the UK and internationally. In 2011 and 2013 I was proudly Scotland's Food Ambassador during Tartan Week in New York and Toronto. I have delivered several banquets in London for charitable organisations as well as my home city of Inverness. For the last two years, I have been commissioned to deliver a St Andrew's Day banquet in Monte Carlo, each attended by HSH Prince Albert. In 2012 I had the honour of representing my country for the third time on BBC's Great British Menu, most notably this time, winning the main course place at the final banquet with the African inspired 'I love kids...' goat tagine.

I'm now permanently based on Skye with my wife Laurence and two children Margot and Ozzie. I'm never happier than cooking at the stoves, continually developing new dishes with head chef Kevin Maclean.

Colbost House, Dunvegan, Isle of Skye, IV55 8ZT.
01470 511 258 www.threechimneys.co.uk

274 SCARISTA HOUSE

Scarista, Isle of Harris, HS3 3HX

01859 550 238
www.scaristahouse.com Twitter: @ScaristaHouse

Scarista House is a comfortable, elegant, small hotel and restaurant on the west coast of the Isle of Harris, with lovely views of the Atlantic Ocean, heather covered mountains, and a three mile shell-sand beach. Harris is the most beautiful of the remote, windswept Outer Hebrides, a chain of more than 200 islands which lie off Scotland's north west coast.

There has been a tradition of hospitality at Scarista House for over two hundred years. In former times, the minister who lived in this Georgian manse would have played host to visiting members of his congregation. Now visitors come to enjoy traditional comfort in elegantly furnished guest rooms, and to relish natural, skilled cooking and good wines in the intimate dining rooms.

Chefs Tim and Patricia Martin carefully source organic, local or home grown produce whenever possible. The hotel's garden provides salad, herbs and vegetables in season. Bread, cakes, biscuits, jams, marmalade, ice cream and chocolates are all made on the premises. Meat is free-range and, when possible, from animals reared on the island. Fish and shellfish are also from Hebridean waters and a local diver supplies scallops. Langoustines (or prawns as they call them on Harris) are delivered the day they are caught in the Minch. Donnie at Harbour Seafoods in Stornoway phones when the local boats have landed and he'll then send whatever is available down on the bus!

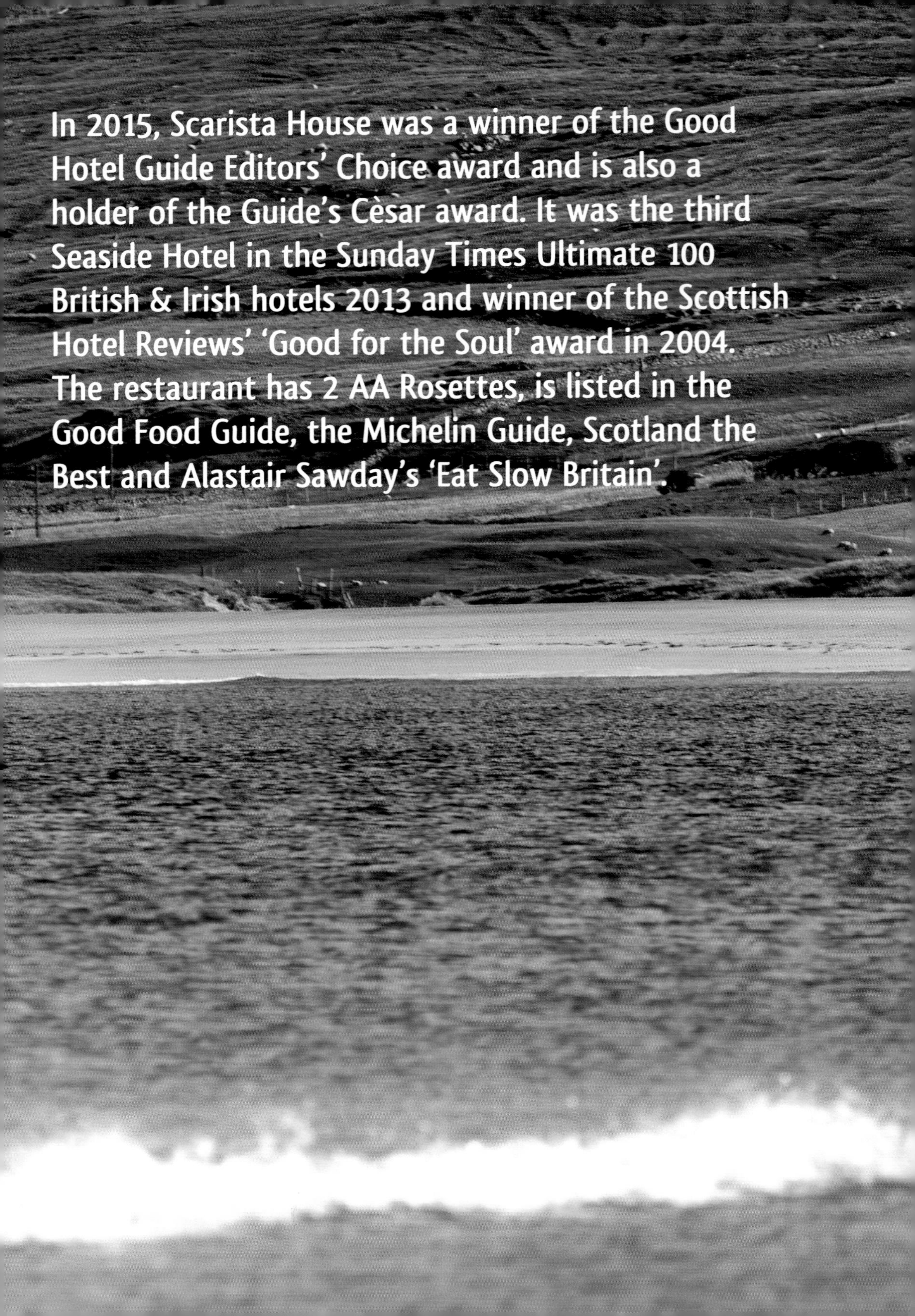

In 2015, Scarista House was a winner of the Good Hotel Guide Editors' Choice award and is also a holder of the Guide's Cèsar award. It was the third Seaside Hotel in the Sunday Times Ultimate 100 British & Irish hotels 2013 and winner of the Scottish Hotel Reviews' 'Good for the Soul' award in 2004. The restaurant has 2 AA Rosettes, is listed in the Good Food Guide, the Michelin Guide, Scotland the Best and Alastair Sawday's 'Eat Slow Britain'.

WEST COAST SALAD WITH INVERAWE SMOKED VENISON & QUAIL EGG

SERVES 8

Recommended Wine: Cerasuolo di Vittoria (Italy)
A delicious red wine from Sicily.

Ingredients

24 strips Inverawe smoked venison

Horseradish Cream

3 dsp mascarpone
2 heaped tsp horseradish sauce
1 scant tsp dry mustard

Croutons

4 thin slices white bread
butter and oil (for frying)

To Serve

salad leaves
olive oil, balsamic vinegar, seasoning
8 quail's eggs

Method

For The Horseradish Cream

Combine all the ingredients and stir until smooth.

For The Venison

Spread each strip of venison with horseradish cream and roll up into a mini roulade.

Chef's Tip

The venison can be prepared in advance and kept covered in the fridge until needed.

For The Croutons

Cut 2 circles from each slice of bread. Gently fry them in the oil and butter.

To Assemble The Dish

Dress the salad leaves with the oil and vinegar and season to taste. Place the salad in the centre of each plate and arrange 3 roulades of venison around the salad. Place a crouton on top of the salad. Gently fry the quail eggs and place on top of crouton. Serve immediately.

MINCH LANGOUSTINES, GARLIC & HERB BUTTER, DIJON MAYONNAISE

SERVES 8

 *Meursault Le Tesson, Jean-Philippe Fichet (France), or any other white Burgundy*

Ingredients

80 medium-sized Minch langoustines

Dijon Mayonnaise

2 egg yolks
1 tbsp Dijon mustard
350ml groundnut oil
½ lemon (juice of)
salt and pepper

Garlic And Herb Butter

2 packs butter
4 cloves garlic (crushed)
fennel, parsley, lovage, chervil (bunch of)
2 lemons (juice of)

To Serve

new potatoes (lightly crushed with olives)
green vegetables (steamed)

8 ramekins

Method

For The Dijon Mayonnaise

Mix the egg yolks and mustard together in a large ceramic bowl. Gradually whisk the oil in, a drop at a time, until the mixture starts to thicken. As the mixture thickens, add the oil in a continuous stream. Season to taste with lemon juice, salt and pepper. Divide between 8 ramekins and chill until ready to use.

For The Garlic And Herb Butter

Melt the butter with the garlic. Set aside. Blitz the melted garlic butter, the bunch of herbs and lemon juice in a liquidiser.

For The Langoustines

Bring a large pan of salted water to a rolling boil.

Cook the langoustines in small batches of 8 at a time; drop them into the boiling water, cover with a lid and when the water comes back to the boil, they're cooked. This only takes a few minutes. Set aside. Don't worry about keeping them hot.

Chef's Tip

You can really only do this dish with fresh, live langoustines!

To Assemble The Dish

Arrange 10 langoustines on each plate and pour the garlic and herb butter over them. Place a ramekin of Dijon mayonnaise on each plate. Serve with new potatoes (we lightly crush them with chopped olives) and a steamed green vegetable. As you can only eat these with your fingers, you will need finger bowls and extra napkins.

TARTE TATIN, CINNAMON ICE CREAM, BLACKCURRANT COULIS

SERVES 8

 *Monbazillac, Domaine de l'Ancienne Cure (France)*

Ingredients

Cinnamon Ice Cream

4 egg yolks
100g caster sugar
600ml whipping cream
1 stick cinnamon

Pastry

250g strong white flour
salt (pinch of)
250g unsalted butter
150ml very cold water

Tarte Tatin

110g butter
200g caster sugar
10 apples
egg or milk (to brush)

Blackcurrant Coulis

250g blackcurrants
100ml sugar stock
1 tbsp cassis
1/2 lemon (juice of)

Method

Cinnamon Ice Cream (Prepare ahead)

Beat the egg yolks and sugar until thick and pale. Heat the cream with the cinnamon, then pour over the egg mixture. Pour into a clean saucepan and cook over a very low heat until the mixture coats the back of a spoon (this will happen at about 80°C). Strain the mixture and leave to cool. Churn in an ice cream machine.

For The Pastry

Sift the flour and salt into a ceramic bowl.

Cut the butter into small pieces and mix into the flour with a knife.

Add the water and mix with the knife until mixture comes together. Shape into a ball, wrap in cling film and chill for 20 minutes.

Knead lightly and roll out into a large rectangle. Fold the top third into the middle. Fold bottom third over the top. Rotate once and roll again. Fold into thirds again. Chill for 30 minutes.

For The Tarte Tatin

Smear a shallow, ovenproof pan with the butter and sprinkle with the sugar.

Core the apples and cut them in half. Place them round-side down in the pan, filling any gaps with cut up apples.

Caramelise to a good brown colour on top of the stove. Remove from the heat and allow to cool. Roll out the pastry again and cover the apples. Return to the fridge and chill.

About 30 minutes before serving, remove from the fridge and brush with a little beaten egg or milk.

Bake in the oven at 220°C for 30-40 minutes, or until golden brown. Carefully turn out onto a plate.

Chef's Tip

By cooking the tart on the top of the stove before covering with the pastry, you can see when the apples have become nicely caramelised.

For The Blackcurrant Coulis

Blitz all the ingredients in a liquidiser. Pass through a fine sieve.

To Assemble

Put a slice of tart onto each plate, a scoop of ice cream on the side and drizzle with coulis.

MICHELIN STAR SPOTLIGHT...

ROSS STOVOLD

HEAD CHEF, ISLE OF ERISKA

This year, the Isle of Eriska celebrates being open to the public for 40 years!

We pride ourselves in the use of the best fresh local produce whether that be fish from Loch Creran, scallops from Loch Linnhe or venison from the hills of Kingairloch. I was delighted that my team and I were recognised with the award of our first Michelin star in 2014. My food is all about flavour and taste, ensuring that our guests enjoy a fresh burst of the ingredients enhanced by our kitchen's attention.

Produce not only comes from the surrounding lands, but also from the Eriska estate itself with a plentiful supply from Eriska's kitchen garden and from foraging on the island and the seashore itself. I work closely with our suppliers to ensure that it is a joint effort to source and deliver the best ingredients for the customer's plate. Whether it be Aberdeen Angus beef from Balhousie Farm or hand dived Mull scallops from Ulva Ferry, their provenance and quality is undisputed. I was brought up through many of the acclaimed kitchens in England and I take pride in my team for their skill at both developing and bringing out the best in the kitchen basket and island larder.

Benderloch, Argyll, Scotland, PA37 1SD.
01631 720 371 www.eriska-hotel.co.uk

286
THE SHIP ON THE SHORE

24-26 Shore, Leith, Edinburgh, EH6 6QN

0131 555 0409
www.shipontheshore.co.uk Twitter: The Ship on the Shore

The Ship on the Shore is located in Leith's stylish Waterfront area and with Murray and Tracey Georgeson at the helm, the restaurant has been impressing seafood lovers for the past eight years. Firmly established as a gourmet destination, the restaurant combines a wide variety of fantastic Scottish fish and shellfish, alongside wonderful game and excellent meat in atmospheric surroundings. A lively, welcoming bar area also offers the restaurant menu alongside a warming bar menu.

When the sun shines, the delicious food can be served outside on the lovely, shorefront terrace beside the Water of Leith. The Ship offers an array of delectable delights from the sea, making it the ultimate seafood destination. Whether for a light lunch or to luxuriate over the Fruits de Mer 'Royale' or Hot Shellfish Platter, the restaurant offers informal, understated excellence. Homemade desserts and fine Scottish cheeses complete a delicious dining experience. Food is served all day from the tantalising menus beginning with classic breakfasts. A crustacea and mollusc menu runs all day, alongside the lunch and dinner menu.

The Ship on the Shore is a member of the Sustainable Restaurant Association and the fish and seafood, which arrives daily, is harvested from sustainable stocks. The Ship takes great pride in using the finest, locally sourced ingredients, passionately prepared and expertly presented. Murray and head chef Peter Mathes have worked side by side for the last eight years. Peter heads up a young, strong, dynamic team in the kitchen with fresh ideas and a fresh approach, which is showcased in the style and flavours offered on the seasonally adjusted menus. Murray and Tracey's approach is warm and simple. The Ship on the Shore offers guests the opportunity to voyage around the culinary experience in an environment of warmth, elegance and creativity.

THE SHIP
ON THE SHORE

Murray, Peter and the kitchen team offer a beautiful balance, between tradition and innovation, using the freshest of ingredients.

CHILLI GINGER & PAKORA OYSTER SELECTION

SERVES 4 (3 OYSTERS EACH)

 *A glass of Champagne*

Ingredients

12 oysters (in shells)

Chilli Ginger Oyster

50ml rice vinegar
1 tbsp lime juice
1 tbsp caster sugar
5g ginger (peeled, finely chopped)
10g red chilli (deseeded, thinly sliced)
1 tsp fresh coriander (chopped)

Pakora Oyster

2 tbsp olive oil
2 tbsp Greek style yoghurt
2 tbsp milk
1 tbsp lemon juice
2 tbsp gram flour
1 tsp garam masala
1 tsp turmeric
½ tsp dried fenugreek leaves (crumbled between fingers)
½ tsp caster sugar
1 tsp fresh ginger (chopped)
1 tsp fresh coriander (chopped)
1 tsp garlic (chopped)
1 tsp fresh red chilli (chopped)
salt (pinch of)
black pepper (pinch of)

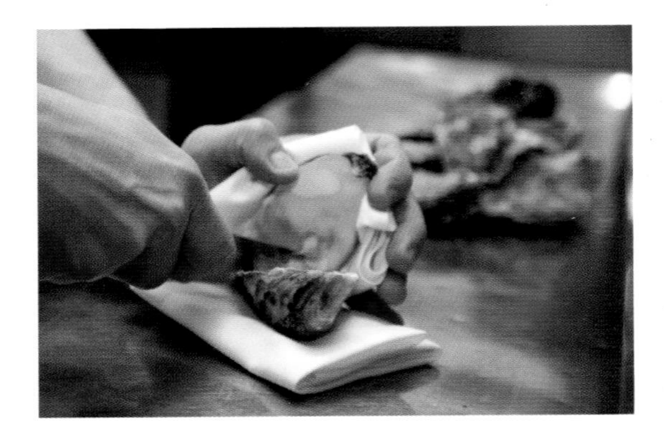

Method

For The Ginger Chilli Oysters

Dissolve the sugar in the vinegar, add the remaining ingredients and stir.

Shuck 6 oysters. Place in their shells on a serving dish and spoon the ginger chilli mixture on top.

For The Pakora Oysters

Mix all the ingredients in a small bowl to give a thick batter consistency.

Shuck 6 oysters. Take out the meat and dry on a kitchen towel.

Wash the deeper part of the shell, dry and place on a serving dish.

Heat the vegetable oil in a deep fat fryer or a saucepan to 180°C.

Coat the oysters in the batter, then carefully place into the hot oil. Cook until golden brown for 1-1½ minutes.

Remove from the oil, drain on a kitchen towel and transfer back to their shells.

Chef's Tip

Get your fishmonger to shuck (open) your oysters for you.

For the recipes for the other oysters pictured: Radish salsa, wasabi crème fraîche, spinach and blue cheese and chorizo and Parmesan, please see our website.

SEAFOOD PIE 'ROYALE'

SERVES 4

 *Chilled White Burgundy*

Ingredients

Fish

4 king prawn tails (shelled)
4 king scallops (shelled)
160g salmon fillet
160g cod fillet
160g smoked haddock
100g lobster meat (cooked)

Potato Topping

1½kg potatoes (peeled)
100g unsalted butter
100ml double cream
salt

Fish Pie Base

300ml milk
150ml double cream
2 bay leaves
30g unsalted butter
50g red onion, 50g celery, 50g leek, 50g carrot (cut into ½cm dice)
30g plain flour
50g garden peas
50g capers
2 tbsp wholegrain mustard
1 tbsp fresh parsley (chopped)
salt and pepper

To Serve

steamed greens

4 individual pie dishes (10cm x 10cm)
or 1 large dish, 20cm x20cm

Method

For The Potato Topping

Boil the potatoes in salted water until tender. Drain, then mash with butter and cream until smooth and lump free.

Season with more salt, if needed. Set aside and keep warm.

Chef's Tip

If available, use Maris Piper potatoes for the mash.

For The Fish Pie Base

Place the milk, double cream and bay leaves in a 1.4 litre saucepan and bring to the boil. Reduce the heat and place the scallops and prawns into the milk. Poach for 1-2 minutes, depending on size. Using a slotted spoon, gently remove the shellfish from the pan and set aside. Cut the remaining fish into 4 portions each and place in the saucepan. Poach for 3-4 minutes. Meanwhile, melt the butter in a larger saucepan, add the diced vegetables and gently fry until tender. Sprinkle in the flour and stir for 2 minutes. Slowly pour in the remaining hot milk from the saucepan, stirring all the time until the sauce is smooth. Add the peas, capers, parsley, mustard and season with salt and pepper. Cook for 2 minutes and remove from the heat.

To Assemble

Place the fish and shellfish into your dish, or dishes, and cover with the fish pie base. Leave aside until set, about 15 minutes. Transfer the potato to a piping back and pipe (or spoon on if not using a bag) onto the fish base.

To Finish

Preheat the oven to 220°C.

Bake for 20-25 minutes until golden brown and bubbling.

Serve with steamed greens.

BAKED BOMBE ALASKA WITH STRAWBERRY ICE CREAM & RHUBARB COULIS

SERVES 4

Tommasi Recioto Della Valpolicella Fiorato Dessert Wine (Italy)

Ingredients

Meringue

6 large egg whites (keep the yolks for the ice cream)
150g golden caster sugar

Strawberry Ice Cream

Ice Cream Base

200ml milk, 400ml double cream
6 egg yolks, 125g caster sugar

Strawberry Sauce

200g strawberries
40g caster sugar
1 tbsp water
1 tbsp lemon juice

Rhubarb Coulis

500g pink rhubarb, 80g caster sugar
3 tbsp water, 1 tbsp lemon juice

Sponge Base

100g unsalted butter
100g caster sugar
2 medium eggs
100g self-raising flour (sifted)

Garnish

icing sugar (to dust)
strawberries

15cm x 25cm cake tin (greased, lined)
5 or 6cm cutting ring

Chef's Tip

The Bombe Alaska sounds a challenge but is simple really and has a real wow factor. To save time you can buy a good quality ice cream and sponge base if needed.

Method

For The Meringue (Prepare ahead)

Whisk the egg whites until they form stiff, shiny peaks and you can turn the bowl upside down over your head without disaster. Using a large metal kitchen spoon, whisk or fold in about a fifth of the sugar - add the remainder gradually.

For The Strawberry Ice Cream (Prepare ahead)

For The Ice Cream Base

Bring the milk and cream to the boil.

Whisk the sugar and yolks in a mixing bowl. Slowly pour in the hot cream, whisking as you go. Transfer back to the pan, over a low heat, stirring constantly with a wooden spoon until it thickens slightly. Allow to cool.

For The Strawberry Sauce

Heat the ingredients gently until the strawberries start breaking down. Blend until smooth, strain through a sieve and chill in the fridge.

Churn the base in an ice cream machine until the mixture looks dry. Spoon out into a bowl and pour 150ml of the strawberry sauce over the top. Fold in, making your own swirls, then scrape into an airtight container and freeze for at least 6 hours.

For The Rhubarb Coulis

Slowly bring all the ingredients to the boil, then simmer and cook gently until the rhubarb starts breaking. Remove from the heat. Blend until smooth. Chill in the fridge until needed.

For The Sponge Base

Preheat the oven to 180°C.

Cream the butter and sugar until pale. Beat in the eggs, a little at a time. Gently fold in the flour. Spread the mix into the prepared tin and bake for 20-25 minutes. Cool to room temperature. Cut out 4 circles using a cutting ring or glass.

To Serve

Preheat the oven to 200°C.

Place the sponge base circles on a tray lined with greaseproof paper and add a scoop of ice cream on each. Fill a piping bag with the meringue mixture and, starting from the sponge base, pipe the meringue all around the sponge and ice cream, making sure that everything is covered. Put the Alaskas back in the freezer if they are not going to be cooked straight away.

Transfer the Alaskas straight from the freezer to the oven and bake for 5-8 minutes, until the meringue becomes a dappled golden brown. Spread the rhubarb coulis in the centre of the plate and place a baked bombe Alaska on top. Garnish with a strawberry and sprinkling of icing sugar.

296 STATION ROAD

The Lovat, Loch Ness, Fort Augustus, Inverness-shire, PH32 4DU

01456 459 250
www.thelovat.com

The Lovat is an independently owned, former Victorian station hotel located in the bustling yet quaint village of Fort Augustus on the banks of Loch Ness. The 28 bedroom hotel is full of character that is carefully balanced by contemporary charm. Over the last 10 years, The Lovat has been nurtured by Caroline Gregory and her team into becoming an award-winning, eco-conscious nimbus that is attracting increasing interest, as well as maintaining a loyal customer base who are captivated by the hotel's naturally warm hospitality in such an iconic location.

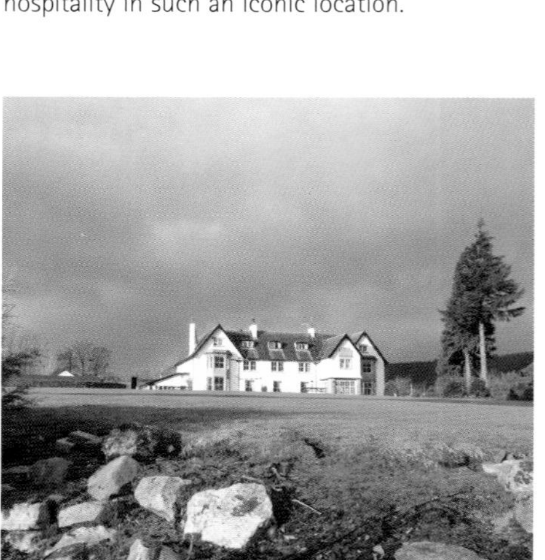

There are two dining areas at the hotel: The Brasserie offers an à la carte menu available throughout the year however, it is Station Road that is the platform to highlight the true talents of executive chef, Sean Kelly.

The AA states: "...there's a lot going on in chef Sean Kelly's world, for as well as being extremely choosy about the ingredients he uses in his five-course dinner menus, he's also incredibly imaginative and creative, producing dishes that never fail to bring a smile to your face..."

Sean is subtly ambitious and adventurous in his creativity, pushing his boundaries as well as yours with his five course set menu. Our 3 Rosette restaurant, Station Road, doesn't offer fine dining - instead we offer FUN dining!

Dining
Room

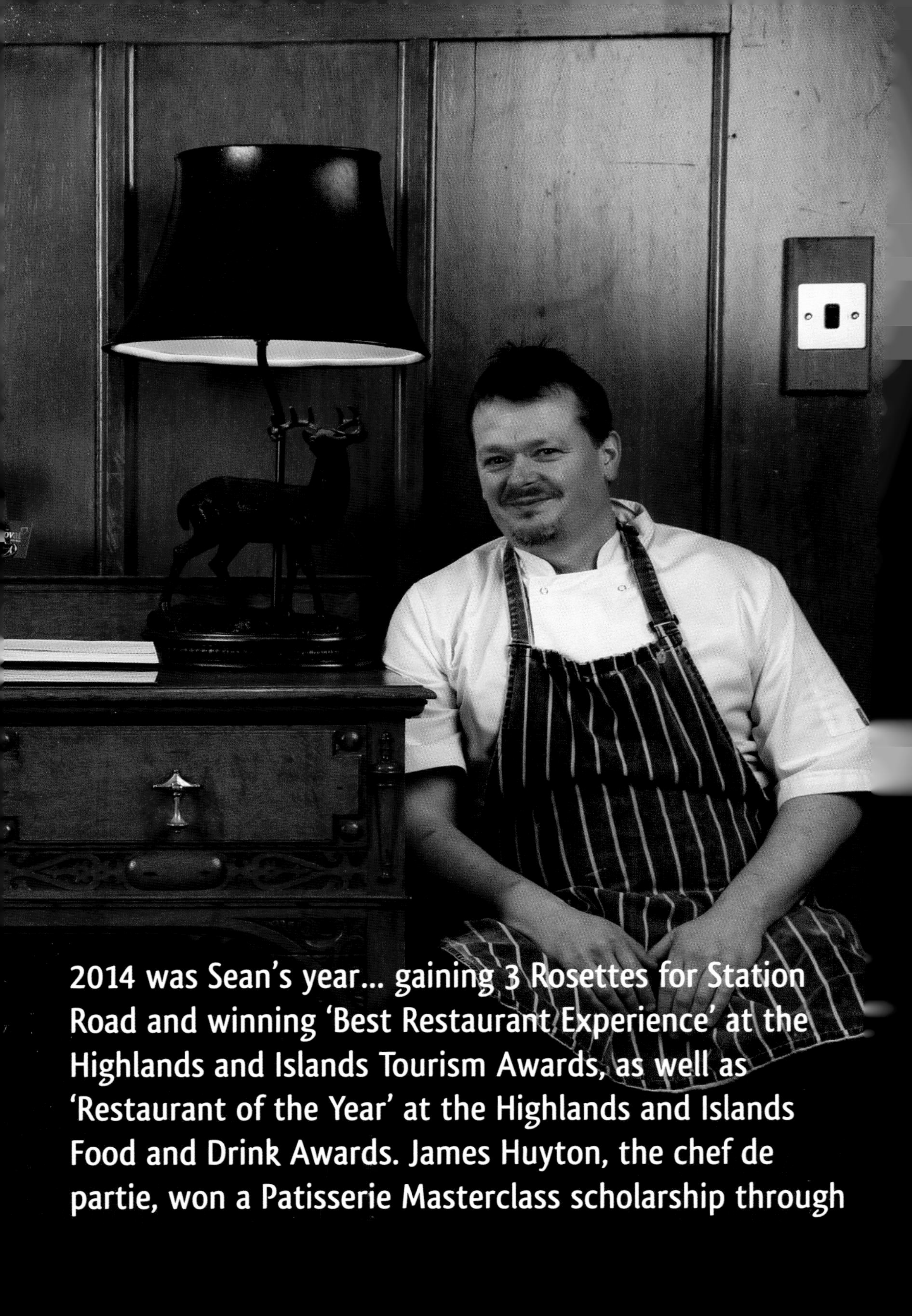

2014 was Sean's year... gaining 3 Rosettes for Station Road and winning 'Best Restaurant Experience' at the Highlands and Islands Tourism Awards, as well as 'Restaurant of the Year' at the Highlands and Islands Food and Drink Awards. James Huyton, the chef de partie, won a Patisserie Masterclass scholarship through

BEEF TARTARE, EDIBLE OYSTER SHELL

SERVES 4

Thiénot, Brut (France)

Ingredients

Oyster Shell

80g dry mashed potato
30g butter
10g oyster juice
1 sachet squid ink

Mayonnaise

2 oysters
100g mayonnaise
0.1g xanthan gum

Beef Tartare

200g good quality Scottish beef fillet
40g shallot (finely chopped)
40g gherkins (chopped)
5g capers (chopped)
Tabasco (a few drops)
salt and pepper

Garnish

sea herbs

4 oyster moulds

Method

For The Oyster Shell

Preheat the oven to 80°C (fan).

Mix the potato, butter and oyster juice together to make a dough. Roll very thinly (paper thin) and cover over an oyster mould. Dehydrate in the oven for 2 hours. Remove from the shell and brush the outside with squid ink. Fry at 160°C for 10 seconds.

For The Mayonnaise

Purée the oysters and add to the mayonnaise. Stir in the xanthan gum and put the mayonnaise into a piping bag.

For The Beef Tartare

Dice the beef fillet. Mix all the ingredients together and season to taste.

To Serve

Place the beef tartare inside the shell and pipe dots of mayonnaise on top. Garnish with the sea herbs.

Chef's Tip

Only use the freshest of ingredients in this dish.

STAG & HEN, SALT BAKED BEETROOT

SERVES 4

 *Velvet, Pittnauer, Burgenland, NV, Organic (Austria)*

Ingredients

Stag And Hen

200g venison saddle (cut in half lengthways)
4 slices Parma ham

Chicken Mousseline

100g raw chicken breast (puréed)
150g double cream
1 tbsp tarragon (chopped)
salt and pepper

Salt Baked Beetroot

2 red beetroot
2 golden beetroot
100g Isle of Skye sea salt
250g plain flour
200ml cold water
1 tsp fennel seeds

Venison Sauce

1 onion (chopped)
50g unsalted butter
100ml red port
1 star anise
1 litre venison stock
salt and pepper

Garnish

cep powder
watercress or beetroot leaves

Method

For The Chicken Mousseline

Gradually mix the cream into the chicken purée. Add the tarragon, and season with salt and pepper.

For The Stag And Hen

Lay the sheets of Parma ham onto some cling film, overlapping them slightly.

Place a piece of venison at the top of the Parma ham and spread 180g of the chicken mousseline next to it.

Roll it up to form a cylinder and tie securely at the ends. Set aside. Roll the remaining mousseline into small balls and wrap securely in cling film.

For The Salt Baked Beetroot

Preheat the oven to 170°C (fan).

Mix all of the ingredients together, except the beetroot.

Roll out the crust to 4mm thick and wrap it around the beetroot.

Bake in the oven for 1½ hours. Allow to rest for 20 minutes, then remove the beetroot from the crust.

Cut the beetroot into desired shapes.

Chef's Tip

Salt baking is a great technique for cooking - try lamb or carrots to enhance any dish.

For The Venison Sauce

Sweat the onions in the butter until soft. *Deglaze* the pan with the port, then reduce until syrupy. Add the star anise and stir in the stock. Reduce to 100ml or until lightly syrupy. Season to taste.

To Cook and Serve

Cook the stag and hen and separate mousseline balls in a *sous vide* at 58°C until it reaches an internal temperature of 56°C. Alternatively, gently poach in simmering water until the internal temperature is reached.

To Garnish

Cut the mousseline balls in half and roll in the cep powder.

Allow the stag and hen to rest for 10 minutes, then carve into 4 pieces and serve as pictured.

(see glossary)

KINDER SURPRISE

SERVES 4

Disznókó Szamorodni, Tokaji, 2008 (Hungary)

Ingredients

Coconut Jelly

100ml clear coconut juice
5g veggie gel
8g caster sugar

'Egg Yolk'

100g mango purée

'Egg Shells'

200g white chocolate

Chocolate Twigs

1 sheet filo pastry (cut into 8 squares)
80g unsalted butter (melted)
20g caster sugar
10g cocoa butter

Chocolate Crumbs

100g caster sugar
100g ground almonds
65g plain flour
50g cocoa powder
65g unsalted butter (melted)

Tapioca Pudding

400ml coconut milk
60g caster sugar
50g tapioca

Chocolate Mousse

40g dark chocolate
1 large egg (separated)
10g caster sugar

Decoration

8 mango cubes
foraged herbs

4 small half sphere moulds
egg shape moulds
wooden dowling

Method

For The Coconut Jelly

Bring everything to the boil and cool to 65°C. It will then be ready for you to use.

For The Egg 'Yolk'

Freeze the mango purée in half sphere moulds and spike with a cocktail stick.

Dip the frozen half spheres in the coconut jelly to coat once, then leave to defrost.

For The Egg 'Shells'

Melt the white chocolate to 31°C and dip the egg shaped moulds, wrapped in cling film, to half way up. Allow to set, then remove the chocolate from the moulds to resemble broken egg shells.

For The Chocolate Crumbs

Preheat the oven to 160°C (fan).

Mix everything together and bake on an oven tray for 20 minutes in the oven.

For The Tapioca Pudding

Wash the tapioca. Add the coconut milk and sugar to the tapioca and simmer in a pan for 20 minutes until the tapioca is cooked.

For The Chocolate Twigs

Preheat the oven to 170°C (fan).

Mix the butter, sugar and cocoa butter together.

Brush the filo sheets with the butter mix and wrap around a piece of wooden dowling.

Bake for 5 minutes, then remove the pastry from the wood.

For The Chocolate Mousse

Melt the chocolate over a *bain-marie*. When melted, stir in the egg yolk.

Whip the egg white and add the sugar to make meringue, then fold into the chocolate.

Chill for 2 hours before using.

For The Presentation

Spoon some chocolate mousse on the plate and cover with chocolate crumbs.

Arrange 2 'egg shells' on top and place a cube of mango in each shell. Place an 'egg yolk' on top in one shell and spoon the tapioca into the other shell.

Finish with the chocolate twigs and herbs.

Chef's Tip

Make sure you use good quality chocolate.
My recommendation is Cacao Barry Inaya™ 65% dark chocolate couverture for the chocolate mousse.

(see glossary)

Marcello Tully
Kinloch Lodge

MICHELIN STAR SPOTLIGHT...

MARCELLO TULLY

HEAD CHEF/DIRECTOR KINLOCH LODGE HOTEL

I arrived at Kinloch Lodge Hotel on the magical Isle of Skye in 2007, moving from Aylesbury with my family. I was instantly stunned by the beauty of the island and overwhelmed by the abundance of delicious produce on my doorstep. Our mussels are picked less than half a mile from the hotel. All of our fabulous herbs and salads are grown in the north of the island. The sea around Skye is full of the very best fish and shellfish and the hills and crofts throughout the Highlands produce some of the best meat and game in the world.

Having such amazingly delicious produce in such close proximity makes my job as head chef at Kinloch Lodge very easy indeed. I have often referred to Skye as a 'Chef's Paradise' and I maintain that to this day. The Isle of Skye is an international 'foodie' destination and has received international acclaim. I feel very honoured to have played a part in this. I was lucky enough to be awarded the island's first Michelin star in 2010 - an Oscar for the food industry.

Kinloch Lodge has been on the culinary map of Scotland for over 40 years - firmly put there by my great friend Claire Macdonald, who asked me to head up her kitchen in 2007. I have always felt so honoured that she selected and trusted me to take Kinloch and its restaurant forward. I have relished my seven years at Kinloch and really look forward to the next seven!

Sleat, Isle of Skye, Scotland IV43 8QY.
01471 833 333 www.kinloch-lodge.co.uk

308
THE TORRIDON

Annat, by Achnasheen, Wester Ross, IV22 2EY

01445 791 242
www.thetorridon.com Twitter: @thetorridon

The Torridon is all about the place and setting. The place is a magnificent former shooting lodge in the north west Highlands, the setting is on the edge of a scenic loch, with a backdrop of one the great peaks of the Torridon mountains. The only thing to distract you from this hypnotic view from The Torridon restaurant, is likely to be the quality of the food which arrives at your table.

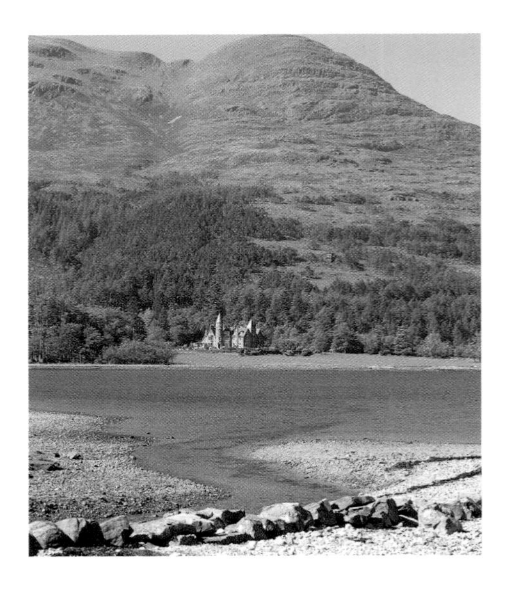

Chef David Barnett is a talented and innovative craftsman who learned much of his trade with Martin Wishart in Edinburgh. However, Barnett brings his own touch to The Torridon table, combining the best ingredients he finds locally with a modern flair which never fails to delight his loyal guests. And what ingredients. From aged Highland beef from the hotel's own herd, to venison from local estates, to seafood fresh from Gairloch, to the remarkable variety of fruit and vegetables coaxed from the earth in the Torridon's own kitchen garden. Barnett has the sort of raw produce to hand many chefs would fillet themselves to find in their kitchen larders. Few, however, have the skill to match his finished creations, whether we are talking about a deceptively simple scallop and crab dish, to a more complex pork pièce de résistance (from their own Tamworth pigs) followed by a brilliantly colourful dessert and intricate, hand-turned petits fours. After which you can only sigh contentedly, push back at your place and contemplate the heavenly setting.

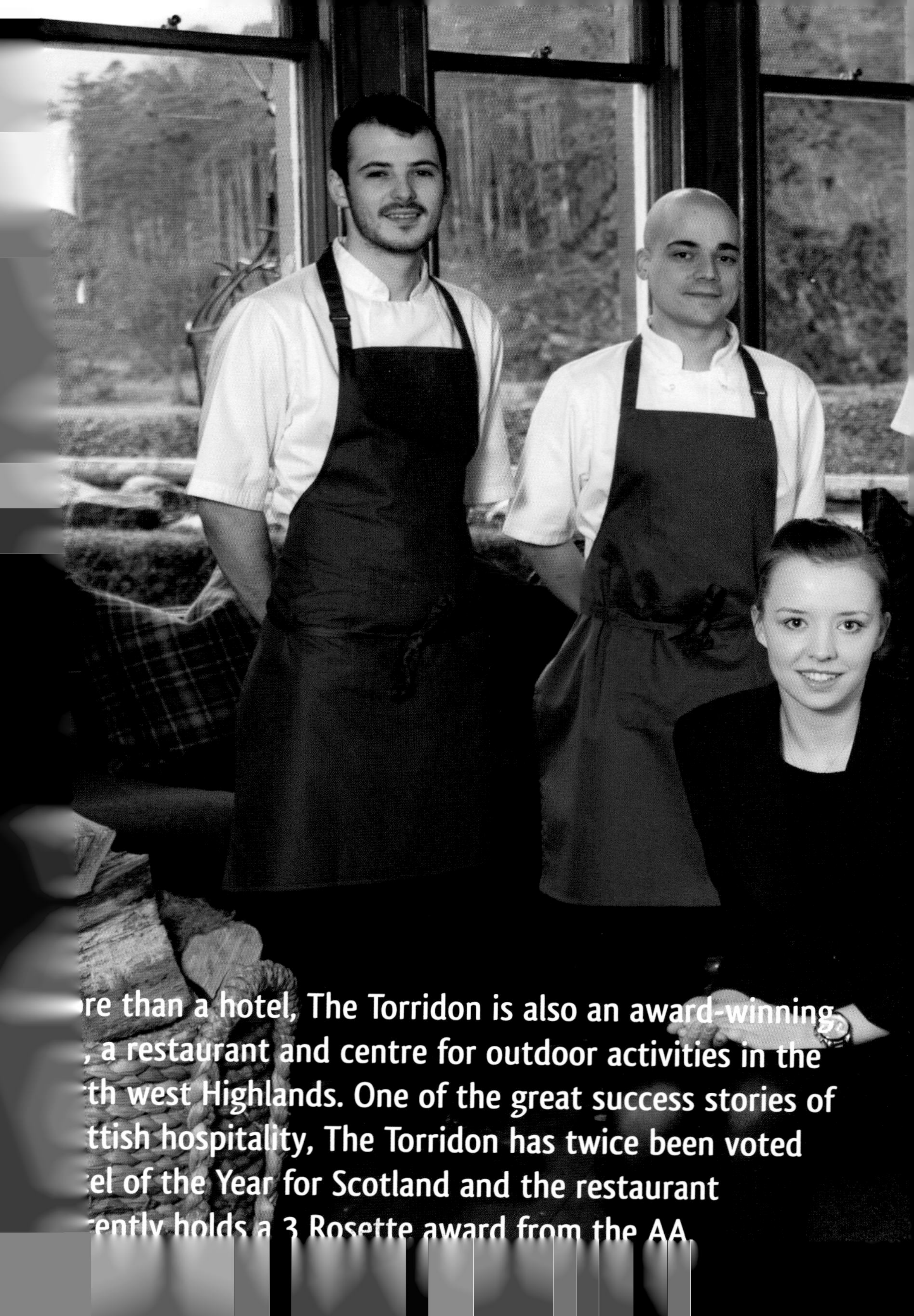
ore than a hotel, The Torridon is also an award-winning
, a restaurant and centre for outdoor activities in the
th west Highlands. One of the great success stories of
ttish hospitality, The Torridon has twice been voted
el of the Year for Scotland and the restaurant
rently holds a 3 Rosette award from the AA.

ISLE OF EWE SMOKED HADDOCK RAVIOLI, SAFFRON SAUCE, LEEK PUREE

SERVES 4

Bogle Valley, Chardonnay, 2012, (Oaked Chardonnay) (California, USA)

Ingredients

Pasta

450g 00 grade flour
2 eggs
4 egg yolks
water (to bind)

Fish Mousse Ravioli Mix

1 egg white
200g white fish (ie sole)
1 large fillet smoked haddock (diced)
170ml cream

Leek Purée

1 potato (finely sliced)
2 leeks (finely sliced)
250ml chicken stock
30g butter

Saffron Sauce

500ml fish stock
2 shallots (chopped)
200ml white wine
300ml double cream
50g butter
saffron (pinch of)

Creamed Leeks

1 leek (sliced)
200ml double cream

Method

For The Pasta

Mix the flour, eggs and egg yolks in a food processor, adding a little water to bind. Finish by kneading by hand.

Roll through a pasta machine to the thinnest setting and cut out 8 discs with a 90mm cutter.

For The Fish Mousse Ravioli Mix

Blend the white fish meat with the egg whites until smooth, then fold in the cream.

Mix in the diced smoked haddock. Roll into 40g balls and place in the fridge for 1 hour.

Chef's Tip

Make up the ravioli mix 2 days before and roll it into 35-40g balls. Leave to set, covered, in the fridge overnight.

For The Ravioli

Take 2 discs of pasta and seal the ball of fish mix inside the discs, using water. Repeat until you have 4 ravioli. Leave in the fridge, uncovered, until you're ready to serve.

For The Leek Purée

Sweat the sliced leeks and potato in the butter until soft. Add the chicken stock and reduce quickly by three quarters. Stir in the cream and bring to the boil. Blend until smooth and pass through a sieve.

For The Saffron Sauce

Sweat off the shallot and saffron in butter until soft. Add the white wine and reduce until nothing remains, then add the fish stock and reduce by half. Stir in the cream and bring to the boil. Pass through a sieve.

For The Creamed Leeks

Gently cook the sliced leeks in the cream until soft.

To Serve

Boil the ravioli for 2½-3 minutes.

Swipe the leek purée on the plate, top with the creamed leeks, then the ravioli. Dress with the saffron sauce.

ROASTED SCOTTISH GROUSE, SAVOY CABBAGE, DAUPHINOISE POTATOES, BREAD SAUCE

SERVES 4

Gigondas 'Parcelles 38', Jerome Quiot, 2010 (Rhone Valley, France)

Ingredients

4 oven ready grouse (seasoned well with salt)

Butternut Purée

1 butternut squash (peeled, sliced)
1 onion (peeled, sliced)
125g butter
salt (to season)
chicken stock (to cover)

Braised Savoy Cabbage

1 Savoy cabbage (cut into 1cm strips)
100g duck fat
2 large onions (sliced)
100g pancetta (diced)
250ml chicken stock
1 large carrot (cut into batons)
½ swede (cut into batons)

Bread Sauce

300ml milk
1 onion (studded with bay leaves and cloves)
1 slice white bread (crusts removed, diced)
1 tbsp Dijon mustard
salt and ground white pepper

Dauphinoise Potatoes

9 Maris Piper potatoes (finely sliced)
300ml cream
100ml milk
4 cloves garlic (crushed)
butter (knob of)

To Serve

Scottish brambles
sauce grand veneur

ovenproof dish (lined with parchment and butter)

Method

Cooking The Grouse

Preheat the oven to 200°C.

Fry the grouse in a large pan until golden on each side. Sit them breast-side up in the oven for 6-10 minutes. Rest for 5 minutes.

For The Butternut Purée

Sweat the onion off in the butter, add the butternut and season with salt. Cover with chicken stock and boil fast until soft and the liquid has reduced by half. Blend until smooth, then pass through a fine sieve.

For The Braised Savoy Cabbage

Preheat the oven to 180°C.

Melt the duck fat in a casserole pot. Sweat off the onion and pancetta, add the carrot and swede and continue to sweat for 2 minutes.

Add the cabbage and stock, season with salt, then cover with greaseproof paper. Cook in the oven for 30 minutes, mixing every 5-10 minutes.

For The Bread Sauce

Bring the milk and onion to the boil. Remove from the heat and infuse for 30 minutes. Remove the onion, bring back to the boil and beat in the bread until smooth. Mix in the mustard and seasoning.

For The Dauphinoise Potatoes

Preheat the oven to 180°C.

Bring the milk, cream and garlic to the boil. Remove from the heat and allow to infuse for 20 minutes, then remove the garlic. Season the cream to taste.

Layer the potatoes in the prepared dish with cream between each layer, up to about 3cm thick. Pour the remaining cream over the top. Cover with parchment paper and cook for 40 minutes.

To Serve

Carve the breasts off the bird. Swipe the purée on the plate, then a spoon of bread sauce in the centre. Top with the cabbage and the 2 breasts. Place the potato on the side. Finish with some Scottish brambles and a classic *sauce grand veneur.*

Chef's Tip

Try to keep your produce as local as possible. You could try the bread sauce with sour dough bread.

(see glossary)

TORRIDON MALT WHISKY PARFAIT, HONEYCOMB TUILE, TOASTED OATMEAL, FRESH SCOTTISH RASPBERRIES

SERVES 4

Bruichladdich 18 Year Old from Islay (Scotland)

Ingredients

Whisky Parfait

8 egg yolks
125g sugar
50ml water
2 leaves gelatine (soaked in cold water)
300ml cream
75ml whisky

Toasted Oats

2 tbsp pinhead oatmeal
2 tbsp icing sugar

Raspberry Coulis

300g raspberries
50g sugar
50ml water

Honeycomb Tuile

50g honey
325g sugar
125g glucose
15g bicarbonate of soda

To Serve

Cromarty Dairy honeycomb ice cream
100g raspberries

500g terrine mould

Method

For The Whisky Parfait

Whisk the egg yolks in a mixer. Whilst the eggs are whisking, boil the sugar and water slowly to 119°C. Pour into the egg yolks and continue to whisk.

Melt the gelatine with 1 tablespoon of the cream and add to the yolk mix.

Whip the cream to ribbon stage and whisk in the whisky. Fold the yolk mix into the whisky cream.

Pour into a mould lined with cling film and freeze overnight. Cut to desired portion size.

For The Toasted Oats

Preheat the oven to 180°C.

Mix the oatmeal with the icing sugar.

Spread out evenly on a tray and toast in the oven for 10 minutes, mixing every 2 minutes, until golden brown. Leave to cool.

For The Raspberry Coulis

Bring the raspberries, sugar and water to the boil. Blend and pass through a fine sieve. Chill.

For The Honeycomb Tuile

Preheat the oven to 180°C.

Boil the honey, sugar and glucose to 145°C in a deep, stainless steel pan.

Add the bicarbonate of soda, mix in well and pour onto a tray lined with greaseproof paper.

Once completely cool, break the honeycomb into small pieces and blend to a fine powder.

Dust the powder through a fine sieve onto a silicone mat in a thin, even layer.

Cook in the oven for only a few minutes - until it's transparent.

While it's still warm, peel off the mat and leave to cool. Break into pieces.

To Serve

Remove the parfait from the freezer and roll in the toasted oats. Plate with a little coulis, a scoop of ice cream, some fresh raspberries and honeycomb tuile.

Chef's Tip

This recipe works best with a good Islay whisky.

318 WEDGWOOD THE RESTAURANT

267 Canongate, The Royal Mile, Edinburgh, EH8 8BQ

0131 558 8737
www.wedgwoodtherestaurant.co.uk Twitter: @chefwedgwood

Since its opening in 2007, Wedgwood The Restaurant has been serving exciting, inventive and unique Scottish dishes in its stylish and comfortable Royal Mile venue. This has not gone unnoticed as Wedgwood has garnered rave reviews from industry professionals, tourists and informed locals and as such, is now considered a 'must dine' destination. A raft of industry awards and accolades back this up with Wedgwood boasting several Scottish Restaurant of the Year awards along with the Hardens guide 'Best New Restaurant in the UK outside London'.

The restaurant is a collaboration between young and dynamic husband and wife team Paul and Lisa Wedgwood. Paul controls the culinary side of things and has a style that is arguably unique. His focus is local and ethical, sourcing only the best Scotland has to offer. He likes to play with classics and turn preconceptions on their head; current triumphs include the cheddar and onion bread and butter pudding with fennel ice cream or the equally experimental lobster thermidor crème brûlée.

His passion for foraging shines through with many wild ingredients knitted seamlessly into the ever changing, tempting menus.

Lisa's style of service is warm and friendly yet professional, slick and unobtrusive. Together they have created a vision of their own perfect night out and they love to share it with you and hope you leave feeling the same way.

Wood

Wedgwood continues to push culinary boundaries and helps to enhance Scotland's gastronomic reputation on a global scale. The dishes are inventive and executed with flair and passion, and served with panache and style. If you don't believe it, then go try it for yourself.

267
DINNER
MENU

LAMB'S TONGUE, BEETROOT, COFFEE ROASTED CARROTS, MUSHROOMS, VANILLA OIL, COCOA NIBS

SERVES 4

Club Altanza, Rioja (Spain)

Ingredients

Lamb's Tongue

4 lamb's tongues
3 cloves garlic (chopped)
1 sprig rosemary

Coffee Roasted Carrots

1 carrot
1 heritage purple carrot
6 coffee beans (crushed)

Beetroot Purée

2 beetroots (cooked)
rapeseed oil (to loosen)

To Serve

75g mushrooms (chopped)
butter (knob of)
salt and pepper

Garnish

vanilla oil (drizzle of)
1 tsp cocoa nibs
lamb's lettuce

Method

For The Lamb's Tongue

Season the tongue and seal in a vacuum bag with the garlic and rosemary. Cook in a *sous vide* for 8 hours at 64°C. When cooked, allow to cool slightly and peel. Refrigerate. Alternatively, gently poach until cooked.

Chef's Tip

Make sure you peel the tongue when it's still warm, otherwise you will make things a lot harder for yourself!

For The Roasted Carrots

Preheat the oven to 200°C.

Place the carrots on a baking tray with a little oil and dust with the crushed coffee beans, cover with foil and roast in the oven for around 20 minutes, or until starting to soften. Set aside to cool. Chop into required shape and size.

For The Beetroot Purée

Blitz in a food processor with a little rapeseed oil, using just enough until you get a nice, smooth paint-like consistency.

To Assemble The Dish

Preheat the oven to 180°C.

Melt the butter in a heavy bottomed frying pan. Dice each tongue into 6 even cubes and add to the pan. Brown the meat, then add the mushrooms and carrots and toss in the butter. Place in the oven for 3 minutes.

Plate some of the beetroot purée in lines on your service plates. Remove the tongue from the oven and season well. Divide the tongue, mushrooms and carrots evenly between the plates. Sprinkle with cocoa nibs. Garnish with lamb's lettuce, drizzle with vanilla oil and serve.

(see glossary)

SESAME ROASTED SEA TROUT, BRAISED PAK CHOI, LOBSTER & BLACK BEAN NORI ROLL, LOBSTER MAYONNAISE

SERVES 4

Fendant du Valais, Jamie McCulloch (Switzerland)

Ingredients

Sesame Roasted Sea Trout

1kg side sea trout
1 tbsp sesame oil
black sesame seed (sprinkling of)
white sesame seeds (sprinkling of)
ground white pepper (to season)
2 pak choi (shredded, centre leaves reserved)
1 tbsp soy sauce

Black Beans

50g dried black beans (soaked overnight)

Sushi Rice And Roll

200g sushi rice
400ml water (for cooking)
35ml sushi vinegar
10g sugar
5g salt
2 sheets nori seaweed
500g cooked lobster (meat removed, shell reserved)

Lobster Mayonnaise

reserved lobster shells (crushed)
250ml vegetable oil
2 egg yolks
20ml sherry vinegar

Garnish

12 slices pickled ginger
reserved pak choi leaves

Chef's Tip

Ensure your sea trout is the freshest you can get! You will also benefit from owning a bamboo sushi rolling mat.

Method

For The Black Beans (Prepare ahead)

Place the soaked beans in a saucepan, cover with water and cook over a medium heat until tender, topping up the water as necessary. Allow to cool.

For The Sushi Rice And Roll

Rinse the rice quickly in a bowl 3 or 4 times until the water is clear. Place in a heavy bottomed pan with the water and bring to the boil. Once boiling, reduce to lowest heat and cover. Cook for 15 minutes. Remove from heat and let the rice stand covered for 10 minutes. Whilst the rice is standing, add the sushi vinegar to a small pan with the salt and sugar and dissolve over a low heat. Allow to cool slightly. Fold through the rice and allow to cool to room temperature.

Spread the rice evenly over the nori sheets, add a line of black beans and chopped lobster meat across the rice and roll with a bamboo mat to form the lobster roll. Toast the outside with a blow torch.

For The Lobster Mayonnaise

Add the crushed shells to a pan with the oil and cook gently for 5 minutes until you get a lobster flavoured oil. Allow to cool.

Blend the yolks and vinegar in a processor. Slowly add the lobster oil until it forms an *emulsion*. Add enough oil to reach your desired consistency.

For The Sesame Roasted Sea Trout

Preheat the oven to 190°C.

Trim the belly and tail from the fish, remove the skin and dice the flesh into ½cm cubes. Set aside.

Cut the remaining fish into 4 even portions. Add the sesame oil to a hot pan, place the fish in, skin-side down, and cook for 1 minute. Sprinkle sesame seeds on the top of the fish and place in the oven for around 5 minutes or until cooked to your specification. Remove from the oven, season with white pepper and allow to rest. Add the pak choi to the pan, adding soy sauce to soften.

To Assemble The Dish

Place the pak choi on the plate and top with the fish.
Carve each lobster roll into 6 pieces and place 3 on each plate.
Add the chopped belly and tail flesh, garnish with lobster mayonnaise and pickled ginger.

(see glossary)

RHUBARB, ORANGE, MINT, HONEY

SERVES 4

Chardonnay Schraube, Umathum, Burgenland (Austria)

Ingredients

Rhubarb Consommé

1kg rhubarb (chopped)
250g caster sugar
1 lemon (juice of)
30g root ginger (chopped)

Mint Granita

100g mint leaves
400ml water
200g caster sugar
½ lemon (juice of)

Honey Jelly

150g honey
80ml water
3 sheets gelatine (soaked in cold water)

Poached Oranges

12 orange segments
300ml Champagne
300ml pure orange juice
200ml water
200g caster sugar
20 pink peppercorns
2 sprigs thyme

Poached Rhubarb

2 rhubarb sticks (cut into 5cm lengths)
300ml orange and Champagne syrup (from the poached oranges)

Chef's Tip

Have patience with this recipe, the end result will be worth it!

Method

For The Rhubarb Consommé

Place all the ingredients in a heatproof bowl and tightly cover the bowl with cling film. Quarter fill a pot with water and bring to a simmer. Place the bowl of rhubarb on top of the pot and leave for 1 hour, checking from time to time to top up the water levels. Once ready, gently pour the rhubarb juice through a fine strainer and let the juice drip through without pushing the pulp. Chill the juice.

For The Mint Granita

Bring the water, sugar and lemon juice to the boil until the sugar dissolves. Chill the syrup. *Blanch* the mint leaves in boiling water for 20 seconds and refresh in ice water. Squeeze the excess water from the leaves and place the mint in a blender. Blitz the leaves and slowly add the syrup. Blitz until bright green. Strain into a container and place in the freezer. Stir the mix with a fork every half hour until completely frozen.

For The Honey Jelly

Line a tray with cling film and place in the fridge. Pour the honey into a pan and bring to the boil until it reaches a dark caramel colour. Add the water, stir and take off the heat. Whisk in the gelatine and strain onto the tray. Chill in the fridge for 3 hours or until set. Once set, cut into small cubes then return to the fridge.

For The Poached Oranges

Place the orange segments in a heatproof bowl. Boil all the other ingredients for 5 minutes and pour over the segments. Tightly cover the bowl and leave until the orange segments are cool. Reserve the poaching syrup for the rhubarb.

For The Poached Rhubarb

Thinly slice the rhubarb lengthways on a *mandolin*. You'll need 72 strips in total. Place in a heatproof bowl. Bring the syrup to a gentle simmer and pour over the rhubarb strips to soften. Leave uncovered until cool.

To Assemble The Dish

Take 6 strips of rhubarb and lay 3 over each other in a criss cross shape. Place an orange segment in the middle and wrap the rhubarb around the orange to make a tight parcel. Do this for the remaining segments. Put 3 parcels in 4 bowls and gently pour over the consommé. Scatter over the honey jelly, then scrape over the mint granita.

(see glossary)

JAMIE SCOTT

MASTERCHEF: THE PROFESSIONALS 2014 WINNER

Jamie, originally from Glasgow, works as head chef at Rocca in St Andrews, which serves Scottish food with Italian influences.

"The 'fantastic chef with a big, big heart' wowed judges with his passion for food." The Independent.

Judge Gregg Wallace delights in saying, *"I can't watch Jamie cook without smiling. He delivers over and over again - the man is just in love with cooking."*

What or who inspired you to become a chef?
My mother was a renowned head chef in Edinburgh and worked for the British ambassador in Berlin and my grandmother was a keen baker. I took inspiration from them and when age 14, I used to help out in the kitchen. It was around this time that I decided to go to culinary college and pursue my dream of becoming a chef.

Where did you learn your craft?
I did numerous stages all over the UK and Spain as well as six years in Arbroath, two years in Dundee and now four years at Rocca.

Tell us about your time at Rocca
I can't praise executive head chef David Aspin enough for helping to nurture me. Rocca has been a fantastic learning ground over the past few years and the team here has helped me to continually improve my skills in the kitchen - it's a fantastic restaurant to be involved in.

What gives you satisfaction in your job as a chef?
I enjoy seeing the results of the hard work of the team and the customer satisfaction involved - putting a smile on people's faces with great food.

Did you enjoy your time on MasterChef?
My time on MasterChef was an incredible learning curve and an emotional roller coaster. I had a little wobble early in the series and all the emotion from the whole competition just completely took over me at times. However, I knew I would have to fight hard to be the winner and was determined to be the best chef in the final. It was a tough competition and the support of my family and the Rocca family helped me to battle through.

For more information on Rocca, see page 262.

CONVERSION CHART

COOKING TEMPERATURES

Degrees Celsius	Fahrenheit	Gas Mark
140	275	1
150	300	2
160-170	325	3
180	350	4
190	375	5
200-210	400	6
220	425	7
230	450	8
240	475	9

*Temperatures for fan-assisted ovens are, as a general rule, normally about 20°C lower than regular oven temperature.

WEIGHT MEASUREMENT CONVERSIONS

1 teaspoon (5ml/5g)	1/4 oz
1 tablespoon (15ml/15g)	3/4 oz
10g	1/2 oz
25g	1oz
50g	2oz
75g	3oz
150g	5oz
200g	7oz
250g	9oz
350g	12oz
450g	1lb
1kg	2.2lb

VOLUME MEASUREMENT CONVERSIONS

55ml	2 fl oz
150ml	1/4 pt
275ml	1/2 pint
570ml	1 pt
1 litre	1 3/4 pt

Relish PUBLICATIONS

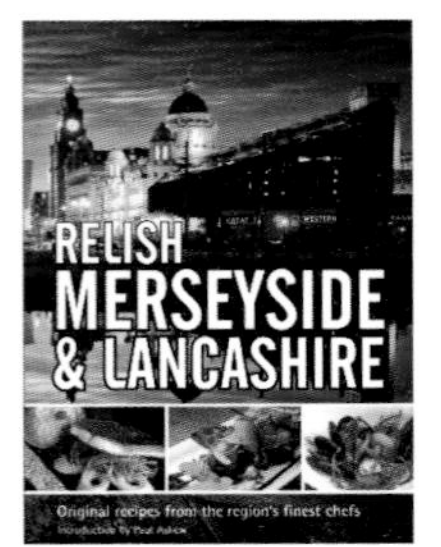

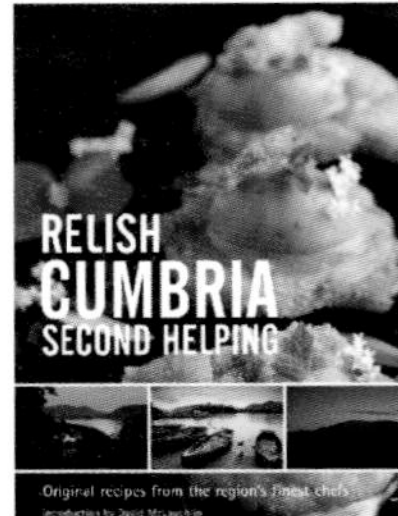

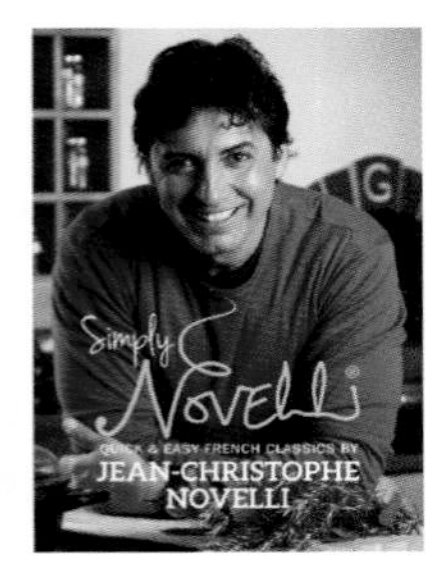

Download your FREE sample pages now from the App Store/Relish Cookbook.

BEST OF BRITISH

Relish Publications is an independent publishing house offering an exclusive insight into Britain's finest restaurants and chefs through their series of award-winning recipe books.

Each book contains signature recipes from your favourite chefs, recommended wines, stunning food photography and an impressive guide to each participating restaurant. These ingredients make the Relish series an ultimate 'foodies' guide for individuals wishing to dine in great restaurants or create outstanding recipes at home.

The series of beautiful hard back recipe books is available to buy in the featured restaurants, all good bookshops and online at the Relish bookshop or on Amazon.

For more information and to read about the benefit of having a Relish Rewards membership (as featured on page 3) please visit **www.relishpublications.co.uk**

Relish PUBLICATIONS

Duncan and Teresa Peters founded Relish Publications in 2009, through a passion for good food, a love of publishing and after recognising the need to promote the fantastic chefs and restaurants each region in the UK has to offer.
Relish Publications also specialise in bespoke cookbooks for individual chefs.

Since launching, their goal was simple. Create beautiful books with high quality contributors (each edition features a selection of the region's top chefs) to build a unique and invaluable recipe book.

As recipe book specialists, their team works with hundreds of chefs personally to ensure each edition exceeds the readers' expectations.

Thank you for Relishing with us!

HERE'S WHAT SOME OF BRITAIN'S BEST CHEFS HAVE SAID ABOUT WORKING WITH RELISH

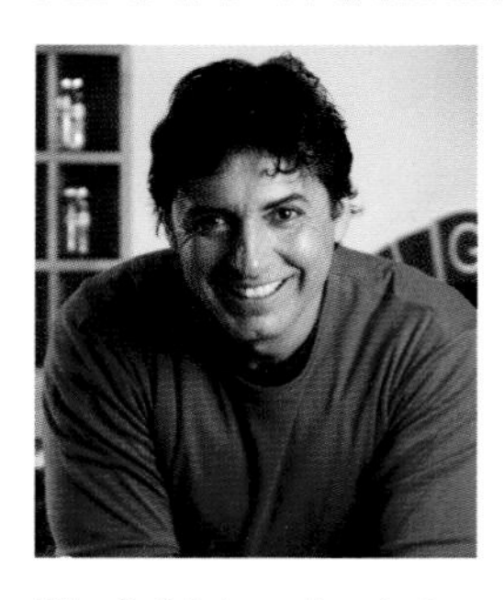

"The Relish team has truly been amazing to work with. To have produced my book within two months from start to finish, only shows how professional a team of people can be."
Jean-Christophe Novelli

"Relish books are full of enjoyable recipes and ideas for making the most edible treasures we have on our doorstep; both places to eat them and new, exciting ways to cook them."
Angela Hartnett, MBE

"Relish Scotland achieves the impossible: it gets better with each gorgeous edition. This third collection is brimming with exciting recipes from a wealth of culinary talent, with magnificent ingredients shining from every page."
Geoffrey Smeddle

"With mouth-watering, easy to follow recipes and beautiful photography, this book is a must have for any foodie, from professional chef to the inspired home cook."
Michael Caines MBE

332 GLOSSARY

AL DENTE
Al dente describes vegetables that are cooked to the 'tender crisp' phase - still offering resistance to the bite, but cooked through. Al dente can also describe cooked pasta which is firm but not hard.

BAIN-MARIE
A pan or other container of hot water with a bowl placed on top of it. This allows the steam from the water to heat the bowl so ingredients can be gently heated or melted.

BEURRE NOISETTE
Unsalted butter is melted over a low heat until it begins to caramelise and brown. When it turns a nutty colour, it should be removed from the heat to stop it burning. Can be used as a base for butter sauces or added to cakes and batters.

BLANCH
Boiling an ingredient before removing it and plunging it in ice cold water in order to stop the cooking process.

BRUNOISE
A type of culinary cut in which food is diced into 3.175mm cubes. The formal-looking little squares add colour and elegance to dishes.

CHINOIS
A conical sieve with an extremely fine mesh. It is used to strain custards, purées, soups and sauces, producing a very smooth texture.

CONFIT
A method of cooking where the meat is cooked and submerged in a liquid to add flavour. Often this liquid is rendered fat. Confit can also apply to fruits - fruit confits are cooked and preserved in sugar, the result is like candied fruits.

COURT BOUILLON
An aromatic stock made from adding onion, carrot, celery, sea salt, thyme, bay leaf, cloves, peppercorns, parsley, and wine, lemon or vinegar to water and simmering for 30 minutes. It is usually prepared ahead of time, cooled and strained before using. Lemon or vinegar added to court bouillon preserves the colour of salmon and turns shellfish bright red.

CREPINETTE
Crépine is the French word for 'pig's caul' in which a crépinette is wrapped instead of a casing.

DEGLAZE
A fancy term for using the flavour-packed brown bits stuck to the bottom of a pan to make a sauce or gravy.

EMULSION/EMULSIFY
In the culinary arts, an emulsion is a mixture of two liquids that would ordinarily not mix together, like oil and vinegar.

MANDOLIN
A cooking utensil used for slicing and for cutting juliennes. Slices can be very thin and be made very quickly. It ensures that all slices are uniform.

MIREPOIX
Finely diced combination of celery (pascal, celery or celeriac), onions and carrots. There are many regional mirepoix variations, which can sometimes be just one of these ingredients, or include additional spices creating a rich, flavoursome base to sauces or stews.

PANNE
To coat with flour, beaten egg and breadcrumbs for deep frying.

QUENELLE
A finely minced fish or meat mixture formed into small portions, poached in stock and served in a sauce, or as a garnish to other dishes. The term is also used to describe their characteristic shape - a neat, three-sided oval (resembling a mini rugby ball) that is formed by gently smoothing the mixture between two dessert spoons.
A quenelle shape can also be formed from other foods such as chocolate mousse.

SAUCE GRAND VENEUR
A classic sauce recipe for large game. The sauce Grand Veneur (huntsman's sauce) based on a sauce poivrade in which some game trimmings and strained marinade has been added to the bouillon and then finished with blood and redcurrant jelly.

SOUS VIDE
French for 'under vacuum.' A method of cooking food sealed in airtight plastic bags in a water bath or in a temperature-controlled steam environment for longer than normal cooking times. The intention is to cook the item evenly, ensuring that the inside is properly cooked without overcooking the outside, and to retain moisture.